The DISCIPLINES SPEAK

Rewarding the Scholarly, Professional, and Creative Work of Faculty

by ROBERT M. DIAMOND *and*
BRONWYN E. ADAM, *editors*

American Association for Higher Education

THE EDITORS

Robert M. Diamond is assistant vice chancellor for instructional development at Syracuse University, where he directs the Center for Instructional Development and serves as professor of design, development, and evaluation and higher education. Diamond directs the national project "Institutional Priorities and Faculty Rewards."

Bronwyn E. Adam is assistant project director for the "Institutional Priorities and Faculty Rewards" project at the Center for Instructional Development, Syracuse University.

THE DISCIPLINES SPEAK
Rewarding the Scholarly, Professional, and Creative Work of Faculty
Edited by Robert M. Diamond and Bronwyn E. Adam
© 1995 by the American Association for Higher Education. All rights reserved. Printed in the United States of America.

The disciplinary and other statements reproduced here appear with the permission of their publishers.

Any opinions expressed in this monograph are those of the editors and other contributors and do not necessarily represent those of the American Association for Higher Education or its members.

For more about AAHE, see pp. 165-167. Additional copies of this publication are available for $10 each for AAHE members, $12 each for nonmembers, plus $4 shipping, prepaid. Prices are subject to change. For ordering information, contact:
AMERICAN ASSOCIATION FOR HIGHER EDUCATION
One Dupont Circle, Suite 360
Washington, DC 20036-1110
Ph: 202/293-6440 x11, Fax: 202/293-0073

CONTENTS

FOREWORD

by R. Eugene Rice

Director, AAHE Forum on Faculty Roles & Rewards

The publication of Ernest Boyer's *Scholarship Reconsidered: Priorities for the Professoriate* launched a vigorous reexamination of faculty roles, rewards, and responsibilities across American higher education. The Carnegie report was inordinately influential because it appeared at a particularly propitious time: Legislators and trustees were questioning faculty workloads and productivity; the quality of undergraduate teaching was being challenged; and changing financial, technological, and political conditions required a basic reassessment. To provide focus and direction to this mounting concern, AAHE, with the generous support of the Fund for the Improvement of Postsecondary Education, established the Forum on Faculty Roles & Rewards. Under the aegis of the Forum, presidents, provosts, and faculty leaders, sensing the urgent need to realign faculty priorities with basic institutional purposes, joined together and initiated a wide range of endeavors aimed at broadening what was honored and rewarded as scholarly work.

It was Syracuse University, however, building on its own experience and the leadership of Robert Diamond and Ronald Cavanagh, that recognized early on that significant change would take place only if the reexamination of faculty priorities was taken to where the faculty live and work — to the disciplines and the disciplinary home, the department. Syracuse also led the way in acknowledging that a single university could not "go it alone" in changing the reward system in a field, that a nationwide endeavor was needed involving the disciplinary and professional associations. With modest financial assistance from FIPSE and Lilly Endowment and the active cooperation and leadership of Syracuse's own deans and department chairs, Bob Diamond and his associates were able to get a wide range of disciplinary and professional associations to engage in the arduous process of developing, gaining approval for, and disseminating formal statements describing the scholarly and professional work of faculty in those fields. For this significant accomplishment they are to be commended.

Henry James once wrote that true happiness "consists of getting out of oneself, but the point is not only to get out, you must stay out, and to stay out, you must have some absorbing errand." The "absorbing errand" for many faculty, particularly in the large research and comprehensive universities, is rooted in the intellectual substance and the communities of discourse provided by their discipline. The socialization of faculty in research-oriented graduate programs reinforces this narrowly focused commitment. By inviting disciplinary and professional associations to pursue a deliberative process leading to a broader understanding of what "counts" as significant scholarly, professional, and creative work — an enlarged view of the "absorbing errand," to use James's words — Syracuse has begun to move us to the heart of the matter.

Teaching and service need to become public, cosmopolitan, and portable activities.

AAHE's recent efforts to strengthen both the teaching and service roles of faculty are directly tied to the disciplinary content of the field. At the Forum's first national conference, Stanford's Lee Shulman led the way here. He insisted that the improvement of teaching needs to be rooted in the intellectual substance of the field. And so, AAHE's Peer Review of Teaching project is organized by discipline; the assumption being that teaching method and technique cannot be disconnected from a firm grounding in the basic content of the discipline. Taking this approach, the Peer Review of Teaching project is having notable success in working in depth with selected disciplinary and professional fields in twelve research universities.

In *Making the Case for Professional Service* (another recent publication of AAHE's Forum), Ernest Lynton presents a similar argument. The professional service of faculty can be legitimately documented and rewarded only when it emerges out of and advances the substance of one's academic field. If a new initiative on faculty outreach and service takes life — and we need one — it will be grounded in working directly with faculty in the discipline.

The impetus for generating the disciplinary and professional statements on faculty work appearing in this volume has two sources. The first is a pragmatic change strategy: the recognition of the importance of the discipline and the department in the work life of faculty and the acknowledgment that the discipline and the department are critical levers for change, particularly in large university settings. The second source is the conviction that teaching and service need to become public, cosmopolitan, and portable activities, that improvement in the evaluation and rewarding of the scholarly work of teaching and service needs — like research — to be pursued not only within the confines of the campus-based departments where faculty members reside but through the disciplinary and professional associations that play such an influential role in establishing faculty priorities.

I want to acknowledge the courage of the leadership in the disciplinary and professional associations in taking on the disquieting task of challenging established and long-entrenched conceptions of the scholarly work of faculty. Also appreciated are the persuasiveness and persistence of Robert Diamond and Bronwyn Adam that made this important collection possible.   □

Editors' Note

In the preparation of this monograph, there was some debate as to whether or not the full text of each disciplinary statement should be included. While there is some redundancy among them, we believe that the full documents provide a picture of the deliberation of the task forces and a sense of the disciplines that would not be visible in excerpted versions. The full texts provide a context that we believe you will find helpful as you review each set of recommendations.

Please keep in mind that these statements were not designed to be prescriptive. Rather, they are intended to be used as starting points as departments and individual faculty members relate the work in their discipline to the contexts of their department and their institution.

While the documents included in this volume were all completed by groups participating in the Syracuse project, the statement from the Joint Policy Board for Mathematics was supported by a grant from the National Science Foundation and the Exxon Education Foundation. The task force for the American Assembly of Collegiate Schools of Business also received support from Richard D. Irwin, Inc.

We would like to thank the Fund for the Improvement of Postsecondary Education (FIPSE) and Lilly Endowment Inc. for supporting the production of the statements in this volume. We also would like to recognize Syracuse University for supporting the work of this project.

—R.M.D. and B.E.A.

DESCRIBING THE WORK OF FACULTY: DISCIPLINARY PERSPECTIVES

by Robert M. Diamond and Bronwyn E. Adam

One thing leads to another — not always in a straight or uncomplicated path, but sometimes in an interesting, often surprising, pattern. Six years ago, when Syracuse University began efforts to clarify its mission and open dialogue with its faculty around issues of faculty roles, no one involved could have anticipated that those efforts would lead to national initiatives to unify institutional and faculty priorities. Synergy is a remarkable phenomenon. The genesis of the work represented in this monograph can be traced back to one campus's efforts to rethink its mission and priorities in the context of higher education's changing national landscape. The statements that comprise this volume, however, are the result of work by faculty-scholars from across the country and across the disciplines addressing the important issues of faculty roles and responsibilities.

In the spring of 1989, Syracuse University secured a twelve-month grant from the Sears Roebuck Foundation to support a project called "Affecting Priorities at a Research Institution: Focus on Teaching." Directors of the project were Ronald Cavanagh, vice president for undergraduate studies, and Robert Diamond, assistant vice chancellor for instructional development. The goal of the Sears Project (as it became known on campus) was to enhance the perceived importance of undergraduate teaching at Syracuse. The project had three purposes related to that goal: first, to help deans and department chairs better understand how they influence faculty attitudes and priorities regarding teaching; second, to assist these administrators in identifying activities and resources they could use to influence faculty attitudes and priorities; and third, to indicate ways in which the university's central administration could support deans and chairs in their efforts.

The decision to focus the project on deans and department chairs was based on two factors. First, as administrators, they are pivotal in influencing changes in both programs and faculty attitudes. As faculty leaders, deans and chairs have a direct impact on instructional effectiveness, since their guidance and example influence the level of effort that faculty devote to teaching. In addition, deans and department chairs affect faculty perceptions of priorities and rewards, as well as departmental norms regarding the importance of teaching, and they allocate instructional resources. Second, the size of Syracuse University (fourteen schools and colleges and more than seventy-five

1

departments and academic divisions) demanded that change be implemented systematically. The strategy of working with deans and chairs provided an efficient means of reaching a large faculty population.

Focus on Teaching

If scholarly research and publication was the work that would earn tenure and promotion, why should faculty instead devote themselves to improving their effectiveness as teachers?

The Sears Project provided a foundation for what later was to become the new signature of Syracuse University — the "student-centered research university." In time, the project also was to serve as the base for two national projects. The first, funded by Lilly Endowment Inc., was a survey of perceptions of the balance between teaching and research at 47 research universities.[1] With further support from Lilly Endowment and the Pew Charitable Trusts, that survey was expanded to an additional 194 four-year institutions in all Carnegie classifications.

The second project, "Priorities at Research Universities: Focus on Teaching," was supported by the Fund for the Improvement of Postsecondary Education (FIPSE) and was directed by Alton Roberts, director of instructional design at Syracuse. In it, teams from six research institutions (University of California-Berkeley, Carnegie Mellon University, University of Massachusetts at Amherst, University of Michigan, Northwestern University, and The Ohio State University) explored the model used at Syracuse and then developed a process for change in their own settings. (Over the three years of this Focus on Teaching project, the campus team leaders also formed a strong network that supported itself and provided information and support to other institutions interested in promoting teaching on their campuses.)

Changing Priorities

Early in the work at Syracuse, faculty comments led project directors to understand that if institutions were to expect faculty to invest heavily in undergraduate teaching, they needed to address the focus on research activity that dominated the faculty reward system. If scholarly research and publication was the

---

1. Peter J. Gray, Robert C. Froh, and Robert M. Diamond, *A National Study of Research Universities on the Balance Between Research and Undergraduate Teaching* (Syracuse, NY: Center for Instructional Development, Syracuse University, March 1992).

work that would earn tenure and promotion, why should faculty instead devote themselves to improving their effectiveness as teachers?

In addition to this concern, faculty stressed that the rewards and recognition system in place in their disciplines influenced strongly how they allocated their time. For many faculty, it was the standards and expectations of the discipline and not the priorities of the institution that determined their priorities. Their identification with the academic field tended to be primary; their sense of themselves as faculty at a given institution, secondary. That this influence of the disciplines was a key factor was reinforced in the first meeting of the teams from the six campuses participating in the FIPSE project. At that meeting, the project directors were encouraged to explore ways to involve the disciplines in any effort to make teaching and applied faculty work more important.

To do so, a better understanding of this nexus of disciplinary and institutional influences over faculty work was needed, and so the second-year continuation proposal to FIPSE included funds to support work with selected disciplines. The project that evolved, "Institutional Priorities and Faculty Rewards," directed by Robert Diamond (assisted by Bronwyn Adam), provided modest stipends, as needed, to support disciplinary associations to develop and disseminate statements describing the scholarly and professional work of faculty in their fields. The statements reproduced in this monograph are the products of our project.

CHANGING THE SYSTEM FROM WITHIN

Recruiting the Disciplines

Our plan was to contact a dozen disciplinary associations representing the sciences, social sciences, humanities, fine arts, and professions, with the hope that six would agree to participate. Deans and department chairs at Syracuse helped us to identify the professional or scholarly associations and appropriate contact persons. The initial contact was by phone, followed by a mailing of descriptive materials. We suggested that to improve communication a faculty member from Syracuse (often a dean or department chair) serve as cochair of the disciplinary statement task force.

For some disciplines, identifying the appropriate association was relatively easy; for others, it was not. Large fields, such as education, have multiple professional associations. In other disciplines, such as psychology, schisms in the profession have resulted in faculty in the field belonging to more than one association. In such an environment, no matter which group was invited to participate, a subset of faculty would claim that the project was working with the "wrong" association. For some of the professional fields — the arts and business, for example — the key disciplinary group was not a "scholarly" society but an accreditation association. As might be expected, this added a whole new dimension. In addition to disciplinary accreditation groups, we were encouraged by the disciplinary associations to include representatives of regional accrediting bodies, since their standards also influence faculty values.

As conversations with the associations began, we realized that there was stronger support from the disciplines than we anticipated. In fact, ten of the original twelve invitees participated in one way or another. The scope of the project expanded even further when other associations hearing about it asked to participate, too. Fortunately, Lilly Endowment recognized the importance of the work and was willing to provide funding beyond the FIPSE support to allow more than six disciplines to become involved. The number of academic areas represented was further increased when the National Office for Arts Accreditation task force expanded to cover all six of its member-association disciplines (landscape architecture, architecture, art and design, dance, music, and theater).

The Challenge of Politics

As the project got under way, disagreements arose within the participating groups about who should be responsible for establishing the task force and drafting the statement. Some associations involved both their teaching and research divisions, while other associations assigned the task to one or another unit. Depending on the association, such assignments made the process of assembling a task force and drafting a statement that members of the association would accept more or less problematic.

The politics of disciplinary groups proved interesting. In some disciplines, the decision to participate in the project was subject to a complicated protocol established by the association for such decisions. In other disciplines, conflict within the association complicated the question of whether to participate or not. In one case, an association's board voted not to participate because it felt that the current definition of scholarship was fine and the emphasis on research and publication appropriate. In another field, as an officer of that association wrote, "Since the board has steadfastly refused to define what [a professional in this field] is, I do not believe that it will be willing to describe what [a professional in this field] does." He was correct.

In some associations, there was a degree of tentativeness. Certain boards were willing to "participate" but held off agreeing in advance to any statement until their task force had finished its work. Others chose to be "observers" of the project. We welcomed such groups, believing that all could benefit from the input of more cautious types.

Certain objections we anticipated. Some faculty, particularly those in the natural and social sciences at research universities, were concerned that any new statement on the work of faculty in the field could pose a threat to the status quo and thus to the resources currently available to them. Members of one group referred to initiatives such as ours as part of "the high-schoolization of scholarship." In some cases, the composition of the association's board of directors — mainly the presence of senior faculty from prominent research universities — had a direct impact on how the association reacted to the project. Some associations reported that their board represents the most traditional cohort of their membership. In another case, after meeting and discussing faculty work, the task force itself could not agree whether or not to produce a statement.

Some faculty were concerned that any new statement on the work of faculty in the field could pose a threat to the status quo.

Building on Other Initiatives

With Ernest Boyer's *Scholarship Reconsidered* widely known, the idea of broadening the definition of scholarly work was not new. Two participating associations had already begun to address issues of faculty roles and rewards when we approached them. The Modern Language Association had established a task force to look at the area of applied work and service, and the Joint Policy Board for Mathematics had established a Committee on Professional Recognition and Rewards. While these associations did not receive project stipends, members of both groups did participate in project activities and their statements, much like the others', address faculty work in the field and how that work should be valued in the faculty reward system. (Only the JPBM statement is excerpted here.)

Participating in the Process

While each disciplinary association had complete discretion in the process of establishing a task force and drafting a statement on faculty work in its own way, the project did provide general, but important, guiding principles:

▶ That task forces be appointed with great care. We asked that members be selected who (1) were recognized in the field as disciplinary experts and (2) would have credibility with faculty-scholars. We also asked that they be selected from an appropriate range of institution types.

▶ That statements be descriptive, *not* prescriptive. The documents were to recognize the contexts within which they would be applied and to encourage academic departments to develop a priority system that was appropriate for their own institution.

▶ That draft statements be widely circulated. With few exceptions, drafts were disseminated by the task forces to the membership for discussion, and then returned to the task forces for revision. In some cases, sessions were set aside at regional and national meetings for this purpose. In others, the draft statements were published and then, based on the comments received, revised for board approval.

Throughout the process, project activities and occasions provided opportunities for disciplines to share documents with one another and to discuss problems and issues. This work brought together representatives from various places in the disciplines. Liaisons to the project included officers of the associations and faculty members designated by their boards, as well as professional staff members (directors or associate directors). This variety of perspectives proved beneficial to thoughtful consideration of the issues of faculty roles and rewards. The process of working with a wide range of scholars yielded a deeper understanding of the complex and dynamic interplay of factors influencing faulty work. For any campus rethinking its reward system, it is important to acknowledge the various factors that converge around faculty as they make choices about how to invest their time and energy.

FACTORS INFLUENCING FACULTY WORK

While important, what the discipline values and encourages in young scholars is only one set of factors influencing faculty work. In the course of the project, we came to recognize four other key variables that influence how faculty spend their professional time. All five variables and their influence over faculty work change over time in response to situation and context, and their relative dominance fluctuates with the stages in a faculty member's career. Consequently, the focus or balance of faculty work is dynamic rather than static. The diagram *at right* illustrates the forces at work around faculty as they pursue their professional roles and responsibilities.

Department/School/College Assignments. Perhaps most obvious among factors that influence how faculty spend their time are formal assignments. Faculty assignments can be thought of as an outgrowth of institutional priorities enacted at the school/

Factors Influencing What Faculty Do

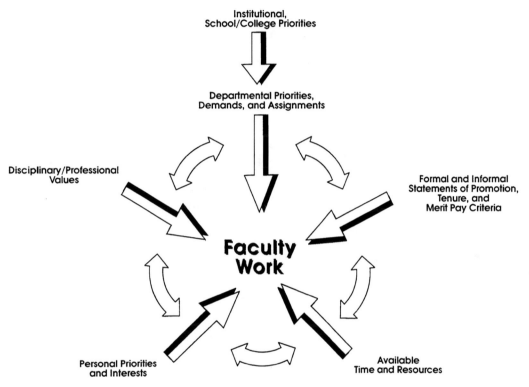

RM Diamond 8/94

college and department levels. These might be imposed on or negotiated with the faculty member.

One of the greatest challenges faculty members face is determining how to spend their relatively few discretionary hours.

Criteria for Faculty Rewards. A second set of variables affecting how faculty spend their time reside in the formal or informal statements outlining the criteria that will be used for making promotion, tenure, and merit pay decisions. Faculty understandably devote their time to activities that promise a payoff for them.

Available Time and Resources. Time is a crucial variable for faculty. The academic calendar presents both a condensed year and many responsibilities competing for the same block of time. Public opinion to the contrary, most faculty work long hours. Workload studies reported in November 1992 note that faculty, on average, work more than 50 hours per week.[2] Time is finite, and the demands are many. One of the greatest challenges faculty members face is determining how to spend their relatively few discretionary hours.

Personal Priorities. The fourth set of variables affecting faculty work are the personal priorities and interests of the faculty member. Given a choice, faculty will gravitate toward work in which they find pleasure and fulfillment.

The Interrelationship of Factors

None of these influences exists in isolation from the others. Values of the scholarly community, as articulated by the disciplinary association, do seem central. They impact on the goals of the academic department, on the allocation of resources for certain activities (particularly if accreditation is involved), and on the personal priorities of faculty in the field. Not surprisingly, faculty educated in graduate programs that are research-oriented tend to enjoy doing research. Faculty attracted to an academic discipline develop the skills that are necessary to be successful in that field. Problems arise when institutional priorities change and faculty are asked

2. Alene Bycer Russell, *Faculty Workload: State and System Perspectives* (Denver: State Higher Education Executive Officers and Education Commission of the States, November 1992).

to spend greater proportions of their time doing work they are ill-prepared to do, from which they derive little enjoyment, or that is not recognized in the faculty reward system.

Also, it is important to recognize that how faculty spend their time varies from year to year, and that this variability may be related to the academic discipline. Often, the nature of the discipline influences the periods in a faculty member's career in which greater emphasis is given to research and/or publication. In some fields, significant scholarly contributions develop over years, as faculty broaden their experience and synthesize the knowledge of the discipline. In other fields, research productivity tends to be highest early in the career, when faculty members are fresh out of graduate school and most current in the literature of the discipline. As professional responsibilities and assignments broaden, keeping up with an area of expertise becomes more challenging. It is also the case that faculty enjoy greater individual freedom in selecting work after tenure has been granted.

Disciplinary societies establish the scholarly traditions and practices that set the standards for the field. Through association newsletters and annual conferences, the discipline groups remain networked with faculty members across institutional contexts in an uninterrupted dialogue extending the length of a faculty member's career. But, at the same time, faculty must work within institutional contexts, and institutions have missions, goals, and objectives as well as cultural expectations and mores. Faculty members·conduct their work within the contexts of these two communities to which they belong and pledge allegiance. To the degree that disciplinary values and practices complement institutional ones, this dual allegiance is not problematic. To the degree that the desires of the institution are in tension with those of the discipline, the faculty member will feel drawn in conflicting directions.

Institutions need to acknowledge the competing calls their faculty hear and work to provide opportunities for faculty to answer them both. Understanding the perspectives of the academic disciplines is the first step in this process.

DISCIPLINARY PERSPECTIVES

A look at the statements reproduced in the sections that follow provides interesting insights into disciplinary perspectives. The participants in the project made clear that, at a quite general level, what the discipline values depends upon what the discipline is *about*. Those differences among disciplines have to do with the situation of the discipline in the academy, and more broadly with its place in the culture and the world at large.

Project Participants

A range of disciplinary perspectives are represented among the project's participants, including fields from the humanities, the social sciences, the sciences, the arts, and the professions. The specific associations that formally participated in the project are:

▶ American Academy of Religion*

▶ American Assembly of Collegiate Schools of Business*

▶ American Chemical Society*

▶ American Historical Association*

▶ American Philosophical Association

▶ American Political Science Association

▶ American Psychological Association

▶ American Sociological Association

▶ Association for Education in Journalism and Mass Communication*

▶ Association of American Geographers*

▶ Conference on College Composition and Communication

▶ Council of Administrators of Family and Consumer Sciences*

▶ Geological Society of America

▶ Joint Policy Board for Mathematics *(excerpt)*

▶ Modern Language Association

▶ National Office for Arts Accreditation in Higher Education,* which includes the fields of landscape architecture, architecture, art and design, dance, music, and theater

(* statements reproduced in this monograph)

Common Interest: The Faculty Reward System

Each of the disciplinary groups had its own reasons for working with the project. One common interest seemed to be that all of the disciplinary groups identified problems for their faculty within existing reward systems. These problems are evident from their statements. For example:

> *Geographers employed in American colleges and universities for too long have been hired to do one job and rewarded for doing another.*
>
> Association of American Geographers, 1994

For history, the privilege given to the monograph in promotion and tenure has led to the undervaluing of other activities central to the life of the discipline — writing textbooks, developing courses and curricula, documentary editing, museum exhibitions, and film projects to name but a few.

American Historical Association, 1994

After reflecting on its study and findings, the Committee discussed at some length a wide variety of possible recommendations. We came to the conclusion that, given the enormous diversity of institutions of higher education and departments, only one general recommendation could be made:

> *"The recognition and rewards system in the mathematical sciences departments must encompass the full array of faculty activity required to fulfill departmental and institutional missions."*

We learned from our study of the rewards structure that this perhaps self-evident recommendation is being implemented in only a small number of departments, and only a somewhat larger number are even beginning to grapple with the issues it entails. There is a clear need for departments to implement the changes that are required to achieve the goal stated in the recommendation.

Joint Policy Board for Mathematics, 1994

Disciplinary Differences

As the disciplinary statements were developed, the differences among the disciplines became apparent. Important distinctions included the following:

▶ No single definition or conceptualization of "scholarship" will be agreed to across disciplines, and to try to establish such a definition could be counterproductive. The task force of the American Academy of Religion described its approach to the definition issue as follows:

> *Given the unique history and place of Religious Studies in higher education, and the diversity of sub-fields, pedagogical goals, and institutional linkages within the scope of the field, we are not at all sanguine that redefining the word scholarship to cover teaching or other professional activities now not normally considered as such is particularly useful or appropriate. Indeed, it could well appear disingenuous seemingly to stretch the categories like this in an attempt to gain what might otherwise be a worthy end. We would rather affirm the importance of excellence and quality in all*

the diverse modes of professional academic work, and redefine or open up the currently operative categories (research, teaching, service) than to create a new meta-category or taxonomy which (a) might eventually not serve its intended purpose, and (b) blur important distinctions within the types of professional work we all attend to. Our report, therefore, focuses on clarifying the scope and variety of professional academic work in Religious Studies — with an eye especially on teaching.

American Academy of Religion, 1993

As the chemistry scholars pointed out in their statement, "it is far less important to worry about what things are called than it is to recognize and nurture important activities." While in chemistry "[t]he words scholarship and research have become nearly synonymous in referring to the discovery of new knowledge," in the arts, "the word 'work' is used in the title's text because it provides an umbrella . . . necessary because definitions of such terms as creative activity, research, scholarship, teaching, and service can be narrow or broad." Encouraging each discipline to describe its work in language with which it is comfortable has ramifications for any cross-disciplinary peer review, such as the present promotion and tenure process on most campuses.[3]

While some disciplines (history and sociology) were comfortable with the four categories of scholarship (*advance, integration, application,* and *transformation* of knowledge) as conceptualized in *Scholarship Reconsidered* by Eugene Rice and Ernest Boyer, others were not. The statement from the American Assembly of Collegiate Schools of Business uses a modification of these categories; other disciplines built their statements around the traditional triad of research, teaching, and service (geography, chemistry, journalism, and religion). Still others, such as the arts, developed a unique schema appropriate for their disciplines. Although certainly complicating, these multiple definitions and schema must be honored in the faculty reward system.

▶ The more comfortable faculty members are with the present reward system, the greater the possibility that they will resist any fundamental change in the ways in which their work is valued and rewarded. It was clear from data in the National

3. Robert M. Diamond, *Serving on Promotion and Tenure Committees: A Faculty Guide* (Bolton, MA: Anker, 1994).

Study (see footnote 1) that many faculty, particularly in the sciences, envision their departments losing resources, and consequently power, if the present reward system is modified. For those disciplines that have emphasized research over the last decade in order to improve their positions in the academy, efforts to broaden conceptions of faculty work can seem dangerously regressive. Engaging such faculty in change initiatives is an important challenge.

▶ Certain faculty activities are more central to particular disciplines than to others. The geographers' statement argues that "[t]eaching is an especially critical faculty role in geography programs for two reasons. First, the integrative and synthetic nature of geography demands clear and coherent exposition. . . . Second, few students enter colleges and universities intending to major in geography." The sociologists' statement argues for the importance of advising and mentoring tasks to their work as faculty-scholars, noting that their "courses attract a lot of non-traditional and underprepared students, and (overlapping but not identical) a high population of minority students." Their statement continues, "[a]s a profession we are proud of these commitments, but recognize the large number of office hours devoted to quality professional practice as advisers and mentors."[4] There are differences among the disciplines that must be honored in faculty recognition and rewards.

Points of Agreement

While interesting epistemological differences mark the disciplines, there are points on which they agree. Project participants agreed that the present faculty reward system narrowly regards faculty work, and needs to be more inclusive in its consideration of the range of work faculty perform. Faculty across the disciplines agreed that teaching and attention to student learning need to be more highly regarded than they are at present in most faculty reward systems. They also came to general agreement about the characteristics of scholarly, professional, or creative work.

Whether it be publishing the results of one's scholarly research, developing a new course, writing an innovative textbook, implementing an outreach program for the community, directing a student production, or assisting in a K-12 curriculum project, faculty on the discipline task forces agreed that there are many activities in which

---

4. *Recognizing and Rewarding the Professional and Scholarly Work of Sociologists* (Washington, DC: American Sociological Association, July 1994).

faculty engage that satisfy the scholarly, professional, or creative dimensions associated with promotion, tenure, and merit recognition. The weight given to any activity is highly context-specific; however, six features seem to characterize that work that most disciplines would consider "scholarly" or "professional":

▶ The activity requires a high level of discipline-related expertise.

▶ The activity breaks new ground, is innovative.

▶ The activity can be replicated or elaborated.

▶ The work and its results can be documented.

▶ The work and its results can be peer-reviewed.

▶ The activity has significance or impact.[5]

CONCLUSION

It is important to emphasize that key decisions regarding faculty rewards must be made at the departmental level, where the mission and goals of the institution, the priorities of the unit, the nature and values of the discipline, and the strengths of the individual faculty member intersect. The fairness of any decision making with respect to faculty recognition and rewards rests on the clarity of the guidelines used, the sensitivity of those making decisions to the differences among disciplines and individuals, and the quality of documentation that is required of and provided by the faculty members being reviewed.

While no single factor determines how faculty spend their time, the influence of the academic discipline is central. It is our hope with this monograph that having disciplinary statements available will support the development of a reward system that is responsive to the needs and priorities of everyone — faculty, departments, and institutions. □

---

5. Robert M. Diamond and Bronwyn Adam, *Recognizing Faculty Work: Reward Systems for the Year 2000* (San Francisco: Jossey-Bass, 1993).

STATEMENTS

American Academy of Religion

RELIGIOUS STUDIES AND THE REDEFINING SCHOLARSHIP PROJECT*

A Report of the AAR Ad Hoc Committee on "Defining Scholarly Work"

PROLEGOMENA

The "redefining scholarship" and "enhancing undergraduate teaching" project has been carried on over the last three years by the Center for Instructional Development at Syracuse University, and has now become a national, cross-disciplinary project supported by both private (Lilly Endowment) and public (FIPSE) money. Inspired by the work of Ernest Boyer (for example, *Scholarship Reconsidered: Priorities of the Professoriate,* 1991) and Eugene Rice (for example, "The New American Scholar: Scholarship and the Purpose of the University," unpublished essay, 1991), this project has been at least initially interested in expanding or "redefining" our understanding of scholarship so as to retrieve, reaffirm, and reward teaching as a "scholarly" activity. As Boyer puts it in the source given above (p. 15):

> a wide gap now exists between the myth and the reality of academic life. Almost all colleges pay lip service to the trilogy of teaching, research, and service, but when it comes to making judgments about professional performance, the three rarely are assigned equal merit . . . the time has come to move beyond the tired old "teaching versus research" debate and give the familiar and honorable word "scholarship" a broader, more capacious meaning, one that brings legitimacy to the full scope of academic work.

In providing a model for such a redefinition, the work of Eugene Rice has been important. In the essay mentioned above Rice sets aside the "trilogy" in favor of a four-fold, overlapping understanding of scholarship and scholarly activity as — in turn — reflective of differing modes of knowing (concrete/abstract, active-practice/reflective-observation). His four-fold scheme understands scholarship as coming, therefore, in four types — discovery, integration, teaching, and practice — roughly consonant with original

---

*Reprinted with the permission of the American Academy of Religion.

research (with interpretations and applications), teaching, and service.

As the project has matured, the national associations representative of the major scholarly and professional disciplines across the scope of American higher education have been invited to participate in meetings and submit reports on the issues as seen from their own particular points of view. Also as the project has matured, broader issues of teaching, teaching evaluation, and service have entered the picture, with the focus shifting from redefining "scholarship" to mechanisms for enhancing undergraduate teaching and its reward structure.

The AAR has been represented in these discussions from their inception. More recently, however, the Board of Directors of the American Academy of Religion responded positively to the invitation to participate more fully by creating an *ad hoc* committee to consider and respond to these issues on behalf of Religious Studies (AAR). That committee, constituted by the membership listed below, met and discussed these matters at the 1992 national meeting of the AAR, consulted with other members of the AAR in 1993, and is hereby submitting its final report.

Ad Hoc Committee Membership
Cheryl Townsend Gilkes (Colby College)
Roberto S. Goizueta (Loyola University)
Yvonne Haddad (University of Massachusetts)
Miriam Levering (University of Tennessee)
Robert Michaelson (University of California emeritus)
Carole Myscofski (Illinois Wesleyan University, co-chair)
Elizabeth Newman (St. Mary's College)
Lynn Poland (Davidson College)
Rodney Taylor (University of Colorado)
Richard Pilgrim (Syracuse University, co-chair)

REPORT

Foundations
Given the unique history and place of Religious Studies in higher education, and the diversity of sub-fields, pedagogical goals, and institutional linkages within the scope of the field, we are not at all sanguine that redefining the word scholarship to cover teaching or other professional activities now not normally considered as such is particularly

useful or appropriate. Indeed, it could well appear disingenuous seemingly to stretch the categories like this in an attempt to gain what might otherwise be a worthy end. We would rather affirm the importance of excellence and quality in all the diverse modes of professional academic work, and redefine or open up the currently operative categories (research, teaching, service), than to create a new meta-category or taxonomy which (a) might eventually not serve its intended purpose, and (b) blur important distinctions within the types of professional world we all attend to. Our report, therefore, focuses on clarifying the scope and variety of professional academic work in Religious Studies — with an eye especially on teaching.

In a recent survey of and report on the study of religion in America sponsored by the AAR and SBL ("Religious and Theological Studies in American Higher Education: A Pilot Study," *Journal of the American Academy of Religion,* LIX/r, 1991; pp. 715-827), author Ray Hart points to a number of important issues relevant to our concerns here, two of which stand out: (1) Even if we do not include professional theological training (seminaries devoted to training religious professionals in a number of religious traditions), religion studies in higher education ranges from theological studies in small church-related schools to broadly-based religious studies in public or "secular" universities; and from small, teaching-oriented Liberal Arts colleges to research-oriented Universities (including graduate studies in religion). (2) Religious Studies, however defined or wherever located, remains suspect in the eyes of many within the rest of the academy, and continually finds itself marginalized or otherwise obscured due to the fact and/or the perception of blurred boundaries between studying religion and being religious, or between education about and education in religion.

These relatively unsurprising but nonetheless important findings (or reminders) should give us pause, as a field of study, (1) in too quickly assuming that teaching is everywhere and always sacrificed to research and publication in the reward structure, (2) in doing anything to further blur the distinctions between professional scholarly (research) activities and teaching or service activities, and (3) in thinking that any particular group or association within the field can possibly speak for everyone. To our mind, the more secure route to enhancing teaching where it needs enhancing (in quality, evaluation, and rewards) is to address it on its own grounds and within its own domain — linked as it surely should be to research and similar scholarly pursuits — rather than lift up through the back door, as it were, by calling it "scholarship."

To the contrary, in fact, we would argue that Religious Studies must continue to present itself as a completely equal partner in the sometimes competing disciplines of academic study by emphasizing its *professional* credentials and its *scholarly* contributions to the general enterprise of higher education. Surely this means, in the larger discourse community of higher education and its very practical reward structures, a continued and explicit devotion to scholarly research and writing — even as we jointly discuss ways of enhancing the teaching enterprise.

More pro-actively and positively, however, we wish to affirm the common and underlying values of the academic vocation, as well as the excellence that should characterize all related and diverse professional academic activities. These activities — certainly to include teaching, research, and service — ideally arise upon the basis of such distinctive values as passionate curiosity, critical inquiry, thoughtful reflection, insightful and imaginative interpretation, erudition and scholarly rigor, articulate expression, and compassionate concern for the communities within which our voice is and should be heard.

These are, indeed, the underlying values of "higher" education in general, and Religious Studies affirms its rightful place within that enterprise — whether it be through scholarly research, compelling teaching, and/or quality service to the multiple and overlapping institutions or communities within which it finds itself. On the basis of these values, then, the three distinctive types of activities arise in a co- or inter-dependent manner — each being mutually enriched and influenced by the others, each being continually stretched and redefined as the living work proceeds in a holistic and protean manner, and each being a facet of the work and activities of the professional academic.

Elaborations

Professional academic activity is based in scholarly intellectual and disciplined modes of knowing, and a commitment to creating, transmitting, expanding, and transforming worlds of learning and understanding. The process emphasizes original, creative scholarship — including research in discovery, integration, and reinterpretation; teaching; and service to the academic institution, the community, and the profession. While we cannot diminish, but should reaffirm the role of research as discovery, we must, in the contemporary situation, challenge the framework of evaluation and reward that treats research and publication as the only valued intellectual activity. In the context of this report, we seek to revalorize teaching to acknowledge once more its importance in our profession, and recommend that special attention be paid to professional service activity such as that which supports our relatively new public forum in the AAR.

Above all else, we seek to inspire and cultivate excellence in all three aspects of our academic activity. Excellence in research reflects the highest quality work, notable in the following dimensions: innovation, integration, creativity, evidence of imagination, advanced language skills, mastery of a difficult area of study, contributions to the field, and communication of ideas. Excellence in teaching involves not only the best integrative and communicative skills but also reflections on and examination of the dynamics of the teaching process. Excellence in service reveals the commitment to the discipline, in integration of personal, institutional, and public service.

Our discussions on evaluation and assessment remained at the preliminary level, but concluded that, as noted above, we value the highest quality work and commitment in all dimensions of professional academic activity. We also emphasize the essential role of the process of peer review in evaluation of the originality, scope, influence, and importance of each teacher/scholar's contributions.

TEACHING

Professional academic activity in teaching is part of our daily lives and forms the cornerstone for our discipline of religious studies. We teach in a field that studies both particular historical phenomena and ontological issues, engaging in philological studies, close reading of texts, investigation of social structures, and the meta-issues of postmodern thought. In the development of critical thinking, we bring our interdisciplinary approach to bear, challenging ourselves and our students not only to analyze our data but also to question the questions — and to ask difficult questions of other academic fields. While we begin with a shared fascination with the religious, some move to consider the most heartfelt issues in personal lives, while others focus on the varieties of religious expression, or seek to transform the understanding of religion itself. Teaching always continues beyond the classroom, and may reach beyond the institution and professional organization as well. The resources we employ are also broadly based; we draw upon not only pedagogical experience and its theoretical foundations but also the relevant facts, interpretations, and issues arising from our research, thus integrating scholarship and teaching. The appropriate means of evaluation and assessment of teaching is grounded in the wisdom of our peers; we must continue working to discover how to reward the already excellent teaching that religious studies professors do.

Teaching activities include (but are not limited to):
▶   Classroom teaching
▶   Computer-assisted teaching

▶ Directing internships
▶ Collaborating with students on research
▶ Student advising
▶ Curricular innovation: developing courses, course materials, software
▶ Development or restructuring of departmental, divisional, or university programs
▶ Development of new instructional techniques or pedagogies
▶ Research, writing, consulting in curriculum and development
▶ Participation in K-12 education and development of materials for such education
▶ Creation of public programs and issues seminars
▶ Course or curriculum assessment
▶ Bibliography or syllabus development for dissemination
▶ Contributions to electronic discussions on teaching

RESEARCH

Original, creative research that advances knowledge is fundamental to our professional activity. Discovery, integration, and interpretation are part of the scholarly work that considers not only the marvelous details of specific case studies but also the history of study and the evaluation of methodology. In whatever area we work, we note that the investigation of boundaries — of study, of culture areas, of perspectives, of methods — is critical to the very nature of religious studies fields. We take reflections on method and theory seriously, and have long grappled with interdisciplinary studies and cross-cultural sensibilities.

Preparation for research in religious studies often entails a broad spectrum of primary source work and linguistic studies, and the differential values of these across the discipline may not be ignored. Research is necessarily a transformative process, affecting the researcher in all dimensions of professional activity and the researcher's colleagues in our own and other fields. Research is especially connected with teaching; the deepened understanding of our research subjects enhances the development and teaching of our own courses and may contribute to the teaching and research of our colleagues. We cannot, then, simply measure outcomes by counting publications. Rather, excellence in research may be defined through peer review and evaluation of many kinds of research-related activities, focusing on the breadth and depth of influence. From this flow various responsibilities to our colleagues and institutions; central to these are our responsibilities to represent the richness of religious studies research, to give and seek support within the existing reward systems, and to extend our transformed understandings to curriculum development. Within the academy at large, scholars in religious studies must not evade but must attend to the evaluation and assessment of colleagues' research.

Research activities include (but are not limited to):
- Original research and theory/method development — disseminated (paper at meeting or conference; museum exhibit; or other) or published (journal article; book)
- Integration of scholarship in review essays, textbooks, newsletters, popular publications, newspapers; through other public fora
- Edited anthologies, journals, dictionaries, sourcebooks
- Critical translations
- Critical editions of documents
- Grant writing
- Creation of teaching materials: manuals, workbooks, study guides, films
- Creation of computer software
- Bibliography development

SERVICE

Professional academic activity in service normally begins in our departments, and extends to other levels of the university or college. Service to the profession, through the regional or national AAR or other professional organization, supports the valued collegial network across which our research and teaching activities may also be encouraged and appreciated. Scholar/teachers in religious studies may also engage in outreach programs of two kinds. First, some may work in community outreach at the local, state, or national levels, providing information on religions and religious studies or consulting on theory, methods, or the central issues of study. Second, some may engage in "applied humanities" service, interpreting or helping make sense of issues that confront the human community, reflecting the best ideas of the field. A scholar might, then, contribute to public discussion on war and peace, on the ethics of suffering, or on the religious history of suddenly-important groups. Excellence in service does not necessarily entail publication in scholarly, refereed journals, hence evaluation and assessment may consider the impact of the activity and its contribution to the enhancement of knowledge and interpretation in the wider sphere as well as to the recognition of our field.

Service activities include (but are not limited to):

▶ Department and campus committee work, in standing, ad-hoc and search committees

▶ Consultancy to departmental or campus committees

▶ Department and campus leadership

▶ Student organization advising

▶ Advisory committees

▶ Professional service: editing journals, newsletters; organizing conferences; leadership in professional organizations

▶ Teaching workshops

▶ Peer review of teaching

▶ Recognition as national/regional authority

▶ Peer reviews of grants for foundations, or articles for journals

▶ Course, curriculum, program, or university assessment, both within one's institution and in service of others

▶ Electronic discussion development or management

▶ Community service, including public lectures or consultancy

▶ Consultancy with the media, textbook publishers, education groups

▶ Media appearances ☐

<u>American Historical Association</u>

REDEFINING HISTORICAL SCHOLARSHIP*

Report of the American Historical Association Ad Hoc Committee on
Redefining Scholarly Work

Despite considerable differences in institutional missions and goals, most American colleges and universities agree on the basic criteria for faculty tenure and promotion decisions: the documentation and evaluation of research, teaching, and service. Although the relative weight given to each of the three criteria varies considerably from institution to institution, critics maintain that too much emphasis is now placed on the research component, with the other two relegated to considerably lesser if not irrelevant status. For example, Ernest Boyer of the Carnegie Foundation for the Advancement of Teaching maintains that this equation of scholarship with research and publication, while perhaps having served many faculty and institutions well over the years, has perpetuated narrow individual and institutional priorities at odds with the broader interests of faculty and with the varied needs of colleges and universities today. In *Scholarship Reconsidered: Priorities for the Professoriate* (Carnegie Foundation for the Advancement of Teaching, 1990), Boyer argues that "a wide gap now exists between the myth and the reality of academic life. Almost all colleges pay lip service to the trilogy of teaching, research, and service, but when it comes to making judgments about professional performance, the three rarely are assigned equal merit. . . . the time has come to move beyond the tired old 'teaching versus research' debate and give the familiar and honorable term 'scholarship' a broader, more capacious meaning, one that brings legitimacy to the full scope of academic work." (pp. 15-16)

This debate over priorities is not discipline-specific but extends across the higher education community. Nevertheless, each discipline has specific concerns and problems. For history, the privilege given to the monograph in promotion and tenure has led to the undervaluing of other activities central to the life of the discipline — writing textbooks, developing courses and curricula, documentary editing, museum exhibitions, and film projects to name but a few. Despite a number of efforts within recent years to give greater recognition to such work, a traditional, hierarchical conceptualization of what constitutes historical scholarship, based on the German university model, continues to dominate and

---

* Reprinted with the permission of the American Historical Association.

restrict our profession's rewards structure. There is little recognition of the diverse interests and talents of today's historians or of the changes that they undergo over the course of their careers. The situation is unlikely to change until we as a profession consciously rethink the fundamental meaning of historical scholarship and the role of the historian as scholar today. While frustration over the academic rewards structure may be the catalyst, a re-examination of the meaning of scholarship has much larger implications for the profession — if scholarly activity is central to the work of our profession, then how we define scholarship determines what it means to be a historian and who is part of the historical community. The AHA defines the history profession in broad, encompassing terms, but is that definition meaningful as long as only certain kinds of work are valued and deemed scholarly within our discipline? If the historical profession is a broad community of individuals committed to "teaching, researching, writing, or otherwise providing or disseminating historical knowledge and understanding" (Report of the Ad Hoc Committee on the Future of the AHA, 1988, p. 1), then the virtually exclusive identification of historical scholarship with the monograph is inappropriate and unfairly undervalues the work of a significant portion of professional historians. Just how many historians are excluded by a narrow definition of scholarship? According to data from a 1985-86 study conducted by the American Council of Learned Societies, only 41.8 percent of historians surveyed have published one or more scholarly books or monographs during their careers.

THE AHA AD HOC COMMITTEE

Within this context, the American Historical Association agreed in 1991 to participate in two initiatives that call for the development of discipline-specific redefinitions of scholarly work. The first, conducted by Syracuse University and supported by the Fund for the Improvement of Post Secondary Education and the Lilly Endowment, focuses on enhancing the status of teaching within the faculty rewards system. Eighteen professional associations are taking part in this effort. In the second project, eleven professional associations have agreed to undertake a variety of efforts to increase recognition for scholarship-based professional service. The cosponsors of this project are the National Association of State Universities and Land Grant Colleges, the University of Maryland at College Park, and Wayne State University, with support from the Johnson Foundation. Those two projects have in turn contributed to a third initiative in which the Association has taken part, the Forum on Faculty Roles and Rewards sponsored by the American Association for Higher Education and funded by the Fund for the Improvement of Post Secondary

Education.

The Association's agreement to take part in these projects rested on five assumptions:

1. That problems associated with the faculty rewards system are not discipline-specific. Hence, individual disciplines and their associations may be a good place to start, but they cannot be expected to bring about reform single-handedly. Similar initiatives must be launched within higher education associations and college and university administrations if there is to be any substantial change.

2. That the AHA's role should not be to prescribe a certain formula but rather to suggest alternative ways of conceptualizing scholarly work and to provide examples of the different ways in which history departments have addressed this issue. The emphasis should be on what "can be" considered scholarship, not what "must be" or "is." Any statement from the Association must be adaptable to the varied needs of different departments and institutions and leave room for individual and institutional choices.

3. That a redefinition of scholarly work should not diminish or undermine historical research but rather extend and enhance it. Nor should a redefinition lead to a competitive situation — the relationship of research to other scholarly work should be viewed as complementary not competitive. Research — as well as teaching — remains at the heart of the profession.

4. That the Association's concern is with historians' activities that relate directly to their research and teaching, broadly defined, and not with public service, civic involvement, or other service to their institutions and communities. While the latter are valuable and should be encouraged, they do not draw upon the historian's professional or disciplinary expertise and cannot be characterized as scholarly.

5. That reform efforts should focus on increasing flexibility within the system and avoid the imposition of additional requirements on already over-burdened tenure-track faculty. Moreover, priorities should change concomitantly in institutional support for faculty. The point should be to change priorities and increase options, not to demand more or increase faculty workloads.

Rather than addressing the two issues (teaching and service) separately, the AHA decided to combine the two efforts into one and develop a more comprehensive statement on the nature of scholarly work and the structure of the tenure and rewards system. Toward that end an ad hoc committee was convened, composed of:

Robert A. Blackey, *AHA Vice-President for Teaching (1991-95)*, California State University, San Bernardino

Blanche Wiesen Cook, *AHA Vice-President for Research (1990-94)*, John Jay College of Criminal Justice-CUNY

Susan Socolow, *AHA Vice-President for the Profession (1989-92)*, Emory University

Philip V. Scarpino, Indiana University-Purdue University at Indianapolis, representing the Organization of American Historians

Noel J. Stowe, Arizona State University, representing the National Council on Public History

James Powell, Syracuse University

Roger Sharp, Syracuse University

Carlin Barton, University of Massachusetts

Gerald F. Linderman, University of Michigan

David Miller, Carnegie Mellon University

James B. Gardner, Acting Executive Director, *ex officio*

A CONCEPTUAL FRAMEWORK

An essay by Eugene Rice, Antioch College, entitled "The New American Scholar: Scholarship and the Purposes of the University," provided the context for the ad hoc committee's work. The Rice essay provides an alternative conceptualization of scholarly work: he proposes that the trilogy of research, teaching, and service be abandoned in favor of a more inclusive four-part definition of scholarship. In so doing, the discussion broadens from issues of balance within the campus-defined function of professor to the larger roles and obligations of the scholar. Drawing on the work of Ernest Boyer, Sandra E. Elman, Ernest Lynton, Lee Shulman, and others, Rice breaks scholarship down into four distinct yet interrelated components:

1. The advancement of knowledge — essentially original research.
2. The integration of knowledge — synthesizing and reintegrating knowledge, revealing new patterns of meaning and new relationships between the parts and the whole.
3. The application of knowledge — professional practice directly related to an individual's scholarly specialization.
4. The transformation of knowledge through teaching — including pedagogical content knowledge and discipline-specific educational theory.

Rice concludes:

We know that what is being proposed challenges a hierarchical arrangement of monumental proportions — a status system that is firmly fixed in the consciousness of the present faculty and the academy's organizational policies and practices. What is being called for is a broader, more open field where these different forms of scholarship can interact, inform, and enrich one another, and faculty can follow their interests, build on their strengths, and be rewarded for what they spend most of their scholarly energy doing. All faculty ought to be scholars in this broader sense, deepening their preferred approaches to knowing but constantly pressing, and being pressed by peers, to enlarge their scholarly capacities and encompass other — often contrary — ways of knowing. (p. 6)

An Expanded Definition of Historical Scholarship

The ad hoc committee then applied this framework to the history discipline, using as a starting point the following passage from the AHA's *Statement on Standards of Professional Conduct* (1992):

Scholarship, the uncovering and exchange of new information and the shaping of interpretations, is basic to the activities of the historical profession. The profession communicates with students in textbooks and classrooms; to other scholars and the general public in books, articles, exhibits, films, and historic sites and structures; and to decision-makers in memoranda and testimony. (p. 5)

That description is clearly broader than the traditional definition of scholarship as original research, and it provided the committee with the basis for developing an expanded list of activities appropriate for consideration under a more inclusive tenure and promotion system. The list that follows is basically an inventory of activities that *can* be scholarly but does not address when a particular activity is scholarly and when it is not — that is an issue of evaluation, as discussed below. For example, teaching can be a scholarly activity but all teaching is not scholarly in nature.

Using the Rice formulation of scholarship, the committee proposes that within history:

1. The advancement of knowledge includes:
    ▶ Original research — based on manuscript and printed sources, material culture, oral history interviews, or other source materials — published in the form of a monograph or refereed journal article; disseminated through a paper or lecture given at a meeting or conference or through a museum exhibition or other project or program; or presented in a contract research report, policy paper, or other commissioned study

> ▸ Documentary or critical editions
> ▸ Translations

2. The integration of knowledge includes:

> ▸ Synthesis of scholarship — published in a review essay (journal or anthology), textbook, newsletter, popular history, magazine, encyclopedia, newspaper, or other form of publication; disseminated through a paper or lecture given at a meeting or conference or through a museum exhibition, film, or other public program; or presented in a contract research report, policy paper, or other commissioned study
> ▸ Edited anthologies, journals, or series of volumes comprised of the work of other scholars

3. The application of knowledge includes:

> ▸ Public history, specifically:
> > — Public programming (exhibitions, tours, etc.) in museums and other cultural and educational institutions
> > — Consulting and providing expert testimony on public policy and other matters
> > — Contract research on policy formulation and policy outcomes
> > — Participation in film and other media projects
> > — Writing and compiling institutional and other histories
> > — Historic preservation and cultural resource management
> > — Administration and management of historical organizations and institutions
> > — Archival administration and the creation of bibliographies and databases
> ▸ Professional service — editing journals and newsletters, organizing scholarly meetings, etc.
> ▸ Community service drawing directly upon scholarship — through state humanities councils (e.g., public lectures), history day competitions, etc.

4. The transformation of knowledge through teaching includes:

> ▸ Student mentoring/advising
> ▸ Research, writing, and consulting in history education and in other disciplines allied to history
> ▸ Development of courses, curricula, visual materials, and teaching materials (including edited anthologies, textbooks, and software) — implemented in the classroom or disseminated through publications (books, professional newsletter articles, etc.), papers (annual meetings, teaching conferences, etc.), or non-print forms

- Organization and participation in collaborative content-based programs (workshops, seminars, etc.) with the schools
- Participation in developing and evaluating advanced placement and other forms of assessment
- Museum exhibitions, catalogues, lectures, film, radio, etc. — public programs as forms of teaching

While the charge to the committee was to develop a discipline-specific definition of scholarly work, the above formulation would be applicable as well to interdisciplinary work by historians. The committee did not address, however, the relative value of or weight that should be given to such work.

WEIGHTING, DOCUMENTATION, AND EVALUATION

As indicated earlier, this list of activities should not be viewed as prescriptive or definitive but rather as suggestive of how historical scholarship *can* be redefined to be more inclusive and multidimensional. While the breakdown provides a good starting point for departmental reassessment of promotion and tenure criteria, any such effort must also take into account the mission and goals of the individual department and the institution of which it is a part. Even if a department adopts the redefinition, it must still determine for itself the appropriate balance among the four components and the relative weight to be assigned to each. A central question that every department should address is whether there is a single mix or balance that each individual within the department must achieve or whether there is room for individuals to weight categories of work differently, as long as the department overall achieves a balance consistent with its mission.

But agreeing on an appropriate definition of scholarly work is only the first step — implementation is impossible without the development of appropriate strategies for documentation and evaluation. Work that cannot be documented and evaluated does not merit reward. But how is the work to be documented? It is relatively simple to provide copies of books or articles produced as part of one's research, but how is an innovative classroom activity or a museum exhibit documented? Advocates of the redefinition of scholarly work maintain that scholarship is strengthened when other activities are included, but it is difficult to demonstrate scholarly quality and rigor when documentation involves no more than counting or identifying. New forms of documentation such as portfolios and reflective essays must be implemented.

Attention also must be given to peer review and evaluation. Who will evaluate this scholarship? Do you require outside reviewers for teaching as you do for research? How do you secure the reviewers needed to evaluate work outside the usual expertise of faculty, such as museum exhibitions and computer software? What will be the criteria for evaluation? In a presentation on "What Makes It Scholarly" at a Conference on Redefinition and Assessment of Scholarship sponsored by Syracuse University in 1992, Ernest Lynton suggested that evaluation criteria might include: the expertise informing the choices made, the appropriateness and effectiveness of the choices, the originality and degree of innovation manifested in the activity, the difficulty of the task accomplished, and the scope and importance of the activity. Lynton's criteria focus on the process of scholarship rather than the product, thus encompassing a wider range of work than the monograph or journal article. For an example of how documentation and evaluation has been addressed for a nontraditional form of scholarship (museum exhibitions), see Thomas J. Schlereth, "Museum Exhibition Reviews: Introduction," *Journal of American History* (June 1989), pp. 192-95.

As each department or institution develops or adopts standards and criteria appropriate to its own mission and goals, the problem of transferability from one institution to another arises — will a scholar with nontraditional credentials find his or her mobility restricted? It is likely, for example, that the most prestigious research universities will continue to weight those activities classified under "advancement of knowledge" very heavily in appointment and promotion decisions. Thus senior members of a department have an obligation to counsel junior colleagues not only about the criteria for promotion in his or her own institution but also about the realities which govern advancement in the profession beyond that institution.

For further discussion of these issues (weighting, documentation, and evaluation) within the broader higher education context, see Robert M. Diamond and Bronwyn E. Adam, eds., *Recognizing Faculty Work: Reward Systems for the Year 2000* (Jossey-Bass Publishers, 1993); Russell Edgerton, Patricia Hutchings, and Kathleen Quinlan, *The Teaching Portfolio: Capturing the Scholarship in Teaching* (American Association for Higher Education, 1991); Sandra E. Elman and Sue Marx Smock, *Professional Service and Faculty Rewards: Toward an Integrated Structure* (National Association of State Universities and Land-Grant Colleges, 1985); and Ernest A. Lynton and Sandra E. Elman, *New Priorities for the University* (Jossey-Bass, 1987). Each addresses both theory and practice and provides additional bibliographic citations. The Forum on Faculty Roles and Rewards of the American Association for Higher Education has assembled a resource packet that includes not only a bibliography of articles and monographs but also a list of unpublished campus documents that address issues of faculty priorities and the reward system. Contact the Forum at the AAHE offices, One Dupont Circle, Suite 360, Washington, DC 20036-1110, 202/293-6440.

CASE STUDIES IN FACULTY ROLES AND REWARDS

For a discussion of these tenure and promotion issues within the specific context of the history profession, see the April 1988, October and December 1989, and June 1991 issues of *The OAH Council of Chairs Newsletter* and the spring 1993 issue of *The Public Historian.* The first and the last provide discussions of promotion and tenure within the context of public history, and the 1991 issue of the *Newsletter* focuses on evaluating teaching. The other two issues present case studies of policies and procedures at eight very different public and private colleges and universities, including a two-year senior college, three general baccalaureate institutions, two comprehensive institutions, and two doctoral-level universities. Moreover, the departments vary in terms of the highest degree offered — five offer the B.A., two the M.A., and one the Ph.D. — and in size — from ten to nearly thirty faculty each. These articles provide both valuable illustrations of alternative faculty rewards systems and direction in addressing documentation and evaluation questions.

The pertinent articles from *The OAH Council of Chairs Newsletter* are:
From the April 1988 issue:
▶   Kendrick A. Clements, "Promotion and Tenure for Public Historians"
From the October 1989 issue:
▶   Donald R. Whitnah, "Faculty Evaluation at the University of Northern Iowa"
▶   Raymond G. Herbert, "Faculty Evaluation at Thomas More College"
▶   Charles P. Carlson, Jr., "Faculty Evaluation at the University of Denver"
▶   Louise E. Hoffman, "Faculty Evaluation at Pennsylvania State University at Harrisburg"
From the December 1989 issue:
▶   Robert W. McAhren, "Teaching Evaluation at Washington and Lee University"
▶   Charles R. Bailey, "Assessing Teaching Effectiveness at SUNY-Geneseo"
▶   Carol S. Gruber, "Evaluating Teaching at William Paterson College"
▶   Anthony O. Edmonds, "The Evaluation and Reward of Teaching: Confessions of a Department Head Who Agreed to Chair a Blue Ribbon Committee on Evaluating Teaching"
From the June 1991 issue:
▶   Russell Edgerton, "The Teaching Portfolio — Recognizing the Scholarship in Teaching"

▶ Peter Seldin and Linda F. Annis, "The Teaching Portfolio"

▶ John Barber, "The Teaching Portfolio: At Last, a Panacea"

▶ Anthony O. Edmonds, "The Teaching Portfolio: A Personal Witness by a Department Chair"

▶ James Wilkinson, "Documenting Feedback in the Teaching Portfolio"

From *The Public Historian*:

▶ Philip V. Scarpino, "Some Thoughts on Defining, Evaluating, and Rewarding Public Scholarship," *The Public Historian* 15 (Spring 1993): 55-61.

For copies of the newsletters, contact the Organization of American Historians, 112 North Bryan Street, Bloomington, IN 47408-4199, 812/855-7311. For *The Public Historian,* contact the Department of History, University of California, Santa Barbara, California 93106-9410, 805/893-3667. □

Association of American Geographers
TOWARD A RECONSIDERATION OF FACULTY ROLES AND REWARDS IN GEOGRAPHY*

FACULTY ROLES AND REWARDS

Geographers employed in American colleges and universities for too long have been hired to do one job and rewarded for doing another. Members of the professoriate have been engaged to teach, but tenure, promotion and salary increases have hinged primarily on research productivity. Until the 1970s, granting promotion and tenure was often the unreviewed prerogative of deans and other administrative officers, and salary increases often were determined solely by program chairs. Many American academic institutions moved to formalize reward procedures in the 1970s and 1980s. As schemes for allocating awards became more bureaucratized, teaching, research, and service emerged as the trinity of faculty roles examined to determine whether candidates should be awarded promotion, tenure, and, in some instances, merit pay increases.

Evaluation of these roles differs in rigor and detail in United States colleges and universities. Assessments of teaching customarily focus on formal classroom instruction and graduate supervision. Evidence of teaching accomplishment consists of student evaluations supplemented by occasional peer reviews. In the sciences, research typically is equated with publication, and peer-reviewed journal articles are accorded highest status. The humanities look for books and monographs as evidence of proficiency, public performance or exhibition is viewed as the mark of excellence in the fine arts, and effective practice is respected in the professions. Service is a catchall for laudable activities that are neither teaching nor research. Often, service is assayed by counting the number of performances given, offices held, and responsibilities discharged, but verification of the quality and the outcomes of service contributions is rare. Research usually outweighs other roles in faculty reward formulae. Teaching and service often are not subjected to the same peer review inherent in measures of research productivity.

Neither American faculty members nor the American public seem satisfied with the priorities explicit and implicit in existing faculty reward schemes. Several comprehensive

---

* Reprinted with the permission of the Association of American Geographers, 1710 Sixteenth Street NW, Washington, DC 20009-3198; 202/234-1450; fax 202/234-2744; AAG@GWUVM.GWU.EDU.

surveys reveal that professors across the spectrum of American colleges and universities question the weights currently attached to faculty roles; they prefer more balance among the three categories and more rewards for good teaching. Society demands much of its colleges and universities, but above all it asks that they be places where undergraduate teaching is an important mission. Many people sacrifice much to put their children or themselves through college, and they — and the legislators who represent them in supporting higher education — expect faculty to be concerned first with good instruction. Both the consumers and the producers of higher education have expressed unambiguous discontent over faculty priorities; in the last few years, criticism has become sharp, even strident.

A consequence of the criticism as well as a catalyst for reconsidering faculty roles and rewards was Ernest Boyer's 1990 report for the Carnegie Foundation entitled *Scholarship Reconsidered: Priorities of the Professoriate*. Boyer proposed to "break out of the tired old teaching versus research debate" by reaffirming the values of teaching and service. He adopted Eugene Rice's four kinds of scholarship: discovery, integration, application, and teaching. Although Boyer's four categories offer useful springboards for rethinking faculty roles, they do not match pervasive terminology, and they engender surprisingly vociferous disagreements among different disciplines about the nature and definitions of scholarship.

As traditionally used, the word *research* necessarily includes Rice's scholarship of discovery — the pursuit and creation of knowledge. Yet, geographers commonly designate as research what Boyer calls the scholarship of integration. For geographers, integrative work may mean melding discoveries in their own discipline with those from other specialties to create larger frameworks of meaning. That integration may be an end in itself, as in a monograph describing a place or a region, or it may be a prelude to addressing a topical problem from a geographical perspective. Those who profess some subfields of geography will distinguish integrative and interpretive work from the research of discovery, while others, in other geographic specialties, will view that distinction as trivial or specious.

Boyer defines the scholarship of application as responsibly applying knowledge to consequential problems. Geographers could interpret that definition in ways ranging from choosing basic research topics that have social and environmental significance to engaging in unusual or even routine problem-solving for a public agency or private corporation.

Boyer's scholarship of teaching relies upon building bridges between an instructor's understanding and a student's learning, and in that process, transforming and extending knowledge. That concept is appropriate for geography, but conventional usage of the word *student* evokes images of campus-resident, tuition-paying, degree-seeking young adults. Geographers also offer workshops for practitioners, seminars for policy-makers, guest presentations in junior high school classes, and other extramural instruction. The Boyer and Rice four-part scheme offers a starting point for reconceptualizing faculty roles, but it stretches customary terminology too far and excludes too much of current experience to be widely adopted.

ROLES AND REWARDS IN GEOGRAPHY

We favor classifying faculty work into four roles that focus on the content of faculty activities in geography. We recognize that each institution has its own ways of defining faculty roles, some open and fluid, some highly circumscribed. In translating the terms we use, each geography program should adapt the concepts proposed below to the missions and nomenclatures prevalent in local evaluation and reward procedures. Where objectives and the ways faculty rewards are tied to them have not been articulated, that task should be given high priority.

Teaching

For the immediate future, classroom and laboratory instruction and thesis advising will continue to be central components of the teaching role. Professing geographers are employed by colleges and universities devoted to classroom instruction. Therefore, they will continue to draw upon their general knowledge of the discipline and appropriate lessons from their personal research to acquaint students in their introductory courses with how the world works geographically. They will use a different blend of general and personal perspectives to lead undergraduate majors and graduate students to progressively deeper understandings of the discipline, its links with other specialties, and its place in society. More often than not, these encounters will occur in traditional settings of classes, seminars, and thesis tutorials. For these teaching roles, traditional reward mechanisms, appropriately rebalanced, may suffice.

Yet teaching has many diverse facets in all kinds of academic institutions. Some of these dimensions common to most disciplines include:

► Advising undergraduates to design degree programs and evaluate career options.
► Supervising undergraduate senior research papers.
► Conceiving and implementing new courses and curricula.
► Developing and experimenting with innovative teaching approaches.
► Designing and teaching courses and programs that integrate geography with other

disciplines.

▸ Initiating and participating in cooperative curriculum programs with other institutions.

▸ Establishing and supervising student internships.

▸ Adapting computer equipment and software to curriculum needs and integrating computer-assisted instruction into curricula.

Some tasks that are particularly important in geography are:

▸ Preparing for and serving in foreign studies programs.

▸ Instructing K-12 teachers (especially important in geography because until recently, virtually no students entered college or university intending to major in geography, and because of the emphasis on upgrading secondary school geography in the 1990s).

▸ Preparing for and conducting frequent and extended field trips.

▸ Winning funding for the specialized computer equipment that is increasingly prerequisite to responsible instruction in geography, and then setting up and maintaining the laboratories containing that equipment.

▸ Teaching cartography, which demands more time per student than most courses, because it can be taught well only tutorially.

Teaching geography involves instructing audiences well beyond traditional, intramural, tuition-paying students. Geographers often find their expertise sought in venues that impose special demands of time and intellectual commitment, demands that should be recognized in faculty evaluation and reward schemes. Faculty increasingly are called upon to convey information and decision-making approaches to the larger communities that provide their students and support their institutions. (The range of such teaching opportunities will be elaborated later in the section on outreach).

Faculty, academic officers, and those who pay the bills for higher education will be more satisfied with faculty reward outcomes if all teaching roles are subjected to peer review. Restricting reward system purviews to traditional classroom and thesis advising responsibilities would be shortsighted, particularly in light of the opportunities for innovative, computer-based, self-instruction that will emerge in the next decade.

Research

Research in geography encompasses three forms of creative work:

▸ Geographers engage in *basic* research to produce or discover new knowledge about the world we inhabit and the ways it functions. In that effort, geographers use an unusual number of conceptual and analytical approaches, drawn from the earth sciences, the behavioral and social sciences, and the humanities. We include in our definition of basic research in geography attempts to enhance the distinctive methods geographers use in their work: cartography, geographic information systems, remote sensing, and spatial statistics.

▶ Geographers who pursue *synthesizing* research seek to (1) combine basic research findings from across the remarkably large number of subfields within the discipline, (2) integrate results from cognate disciplines into geographical analysis and theory, and (3) merge existing and new knowledge about a place or a region into a cohesive portrayal of that area, either as an entity of intrinsic interest or as the locus of a topical phenomenon or problem.

▶ Academic geographers engaged in *applied* research (as distinct from geographers who *practice* in the private and public sectors) focus on solving societal problems. They may pose the issues they address, or they may respond to challenges that arise in relevant agencies, firms, or industries. Although geographers who prefer applied research often apply the results of basic research to extramural problems, ideas flow in both directions between basic and applied research. Basic questions often arise in the course of trying to solve a seemingly straightforward practical problem.

As noted earlier, geographers who can demonstrate proficiency in basic research have an inside track in winning professional recognition and the tangible rewards that accompany it. Those who concentrate on synthesizing and applied research often must work harder and longer for equivalent rewards, even though synthesizing and applied research long have been embedded in the geographic research tradition.

Basic research will persist as a foundation for other kinds of research in geography. Accordingly, geographers should continue to value it highly, evaluate its quality rigorously, and reward it appropriately. However that priority does not imply that basic research should continue to be accorded its traditional weight relative to synthesizing and applied research. Integration and application deserve greater returns than have customarily accrued to them. To achieve that rebalancing, the products of synthesis and application must be subjected to the same intense peer evaluation that is used to assess basic research.

Outreach

Service often has been used as a catchall category to encompass work not clearly included under the traditional rubrics of teaching and research. We prefer to characterize the third major role geographers play as *outreach*. Outreach in geography includes, among other activities:

▶ Responding to requests to undertake applied research projects.

- ▶ Consulting in the public and private sectors.
- ▶ Helping improve geography instruction in primary, secondary, and postsecondary schools.
- ▶ Explaining one's discipline or research using mass media.
- ▶ Writing for lay audiences.
- ▶ Testifying as an expert in legislative or judicial settings.
- ▶ Lecturing to the public.
- ▶ Serving on boards and commissions that draw upon and enhance disciplinary and professional expertise.

Geographers deal with the world as it exists and as it might be. They have much of great value to say about environmental and human problems across a spectrum of analytical scales ranging from localities to the globe. In lending their energies to those problems in ways that draw upon and exercise their expertise, geographers fulfill a mandate implicit in the intellectual heritage they cultivate. Accordingly, outreach should be valued more highly than it has been in most academic institutions since World War II. Individual programs will accord outreach different weights when striking their own balances among faculty roles, but more incentives for faculty to undertake outreach would yield worthwhile dividends, including:

- ▶ Greater visibility resulting from the appreciation by decision-makers and the public of contributions by geographers to the solution of societal problems.
- ▶ Augmented theoretical development engendered by the propensity of the world to work contrary to theory-based expectations.
- ▶ Enhanced faculty proficiency in teaching and research as a result of grappling with substantive problems.
- ▶ Laboratory and field experience for students, including internships.
- ▶ Increased financial support for students and equipment based on better knowledge of agency and industry needs and funding opportunities.

Geography's strong empirical and exploratory traditions and its rootedness in real places and regions often lead geographers to devote considerable energy and time to outreach. The ability and propensity of geographers to grapple with real problems is a disciplinary strength and an institutional asset. Geography programs should ensure that their departmental and institutional reward systems weight such contributions appropriately.

Citizenship

Citizenship obligations accompany every professorial appointment. One way faculty members exercise citizenship is by service within their programs or departments. As the term implies, all faculty members should take some share of common responsibilities. Within any program, tasks should be allocated as needed for the ongoing functioning of the organization. Citizenship at the institutional scale maintains a program's visibility on campus, and individual faculty members also must assume an appropriate share of such corporate responsibilities. Occasionally, citizenship within an institution may draw upon a faculty member's geographical expertise in the same way that local bodies may call upon it. Occasionally, exceptionally large citizenship commitments may be required without significant work reduction, such as presiding over a faculty senate or chairing a major university task force. On such occasions, recognition beyond that accorded to expected levels of citizenship should be given.

A second arena in which faculty members discharge citizenship responsibilities is their disciplines. Faculty reasonably can be expected to review journal manuscripts and research proposals, advise extramural colleagues on work in progress, write letters of recommendation for students and for colleagues, and accept appointments to the committees of scholarly societies. As with institutional citizenship, disciplinary service sometimes may require extraordinary commitments that warrant special recognition; an example would be serving as president of a scholarly society.

The fulfillment of *civic* responsibilities should not be confused with professorial citizenship. However laudable, an activity that is not grounded in disciplinary knowledge, faculty role expertise, or both, has no place in faculty reward evaluations. Speaking about geography to your daughter's elementary school class during Geography Awareness Week may be an instance of citizenship; speaking to your daughter's class about your hobby is not.

Overlap

Teaching, research, outreach, and citizenship comprise a fuzzy set; they overlap and intermingle. The settings in which faculty play the four roles often determine how geographers classify identical contributions. One program's applied research, for example, may be another institution's outreach. General definitions will remain arguable and imprecise, but each institution should have little difficulty formulating its own appropriate conceptualizations, assuming it has clearly articulated missions. Such imprecision and variations do not gainsay the validity of this or any other general schema, or the roles they attempt to encapsulate. Roles and categories are both elements of a coherent process of discovering, refining, integrating, transmitting, and applying geographical knowledge. Teaching, research, outreach, and citizenship — whatever the fuzziness of their boundaries generally and locally — inform and enrich each other. They form a continuum of creative and pedagogical activities that differ less in content and mode than in the locations where they play out and in the clienteles they address.

Distinctive Roles and Rewards

A set of pressing current issues taps the expertise of geographers in ways that should be incorporated into their role and reward schemes. Opportunities and problems arising from the globalization of the world's economic systems and from the linkages between global systems and local business and industry are the stuff of contemporary economic geography. The study of global environments and their connections to human activities in locales and regions persists as the cornerstone of geographic research and teaching. As colleges and universities continue to re-examine and recast their curricula, geography's many ties with cognate disciplines provide special and challenging opportunities to contribute an integrated view to discussions among disciplinary specialists. In pedagogy, emphasis on mapping, field work, and laboratory demonstration augment the traditional formats of instruction in classrooms, libraries, and tutorials. Geographers already employ the diversity of learning modes upon which expanded educational missions of the future will rely. Because of the breadth of perspectives they embrace, geographers already are experienced in what other specialties are beginning to attempt.

RECOMMENDATIONS

1. We recommend that competent teaching — verified by rigorous peer review — be a *necessary condition* of retention and advancement in all professorial positions in geography in all academic institutions. Teaching should be valued more highly in allocating faculty rewards than it has been for the last several decades, especially in relation to discovery.

    All students deserve faculty who are able teachers; ideally they should have access to talented and dedicated teachers. Teaching is an especially critical faculty role in geography programs for two reasons. First, the integrative and synthetic nature of geography demands clear and coherent exposition if it is to be conveyed properly, effectively received, and intelligently acted upon by students, whatever the venue in which they are taught. Second, few students enter colleges and universities intending to major in geography. Almost every one of the 3,000-plus U.S. students who earn baccalaureate degrees in geography each year is attracted to the discipline by an excellent teacher who offered compelling content in an introductory course. Ethics and disciplinary progress demand that good — not just adequate — instruction be a necessary condition of all professorial appointments. Geographers take society's coin for educating its citizens, and their specialty cannot thrive without devotion to that role.

Teaching competence should be verified by rigorous peer review. A variety of measures can be used to assess teaching, including student evaluations, teaching portfolios, and classroom visits by peers. Academic administrators should seek from colleagues or administrators responsible for cross-disciplinary programs evidence of satisfactory and exceptional accomplishment for teaching conducted outside geography programs. We reiterate our recommendation that teaching be accorded higher value in promotion, tenure, salary, and other reward allocations than it has been given over the last several decades, especially in relation to research.

To improve the teaching abilities of future faculty members who will face greater emphasis on quality teaching as a criterion for retention and advancement, we recommend that graduate departments require instruction in effective teaching, especially for doctoral candidates who aspire to academic careers.

2. We recommend that rigorously peer-reviewed research be accorded first priority in allocating faculty rewards in geography programs whose mission contains a major research component. Peer review of research should focus more than it currently does on the quality and originality of research publications as well as on their number. We further recommend that institutions be realistic about their emphasis on research in relation to other institutional demands on faculty time. A chancellor who presses faculty to conduct research in an institution with a five course per semester teaching load has undertaken a fool's errand. The importance of the research component has, does, and will continue to differ among institutions in higher education. Where research is not a primary mission element, the performance of teaching or outreach roles should outweigh research in importance in the allocation of faculty rewards.

Even in institutions and programs whose mission is principally or indeed exclusively instructional, teaching, as scholarly work, should be informed by active research. To profess geography should mean to participate in the ongoing elaboration of knowledge in the discipline. To profess geography is to go beyond being a passive conduit for insights borrowed from others. To profess is to spark in students the capacity for independent learning that is best stimulated by personal engagement, however limited, in original research. Teaching unalloyed with at least some research risks leaving students with only the content of geography and denying them insight into the processes that create that content. We recognize the obstacles to research that confront colleagues in programs with crushing teaching loads. Those obstacles should challenge the entire discipline to convince the leaders of teaching institutions of the shortsightedness of denying their faculty opportunities to engage in the research and outreach that can immeasurably enrich teaching.

3. We recommend that outreach (the traditional service category) be carefully rethought to tease out its distinctively geographic components and that consideration be given to the degree to which they overlap and complement teaching and research. Where outreach in its various guises forms a major component of program and institutional missions, it should be weighted proportionately in the faculty reward equation. We recommend that geography programs:

    ▶   Examine their missions and arrive at consensus regarding the importance of outreach.

    ▶   Develop coherent, systematic plans for evaluating and valuing outreach roles. Those procedures should include peer as well as client evaluation of outreach results.

    ▶   Ensure that the results of outreach roles feed back into teaching and basic research.
    To serve as a basis for faculty rewards, outreach should be rooted in disciplinary expertise and it should be *fertile*; it should differ from routine consulting or practice by offering the potential for deepening a discipline's understandings and expanding the scope of their applications. Faculty should be encouraged to disseminate the results of outreach roles in appropriate ways. When a stint of exceptionally demanding outreach warrants special consideration in the reward scheme, the work performed should be carefully reviewed by an external group of peers who engage in the same kind of work.

4. We recommend that the discharge of normal citizenship responsibilities, whether intra- or extra-mural, not be deemed worthy of special note in allocating rewards. Exceptional contributions deserve consideration appropriate to a program's missions. If institutional and disciplinary citizenship are terms entered into the reward equation, they should be evaluated formally rather than via the informal judgments of colleagues. Assessments of institutional and professional citizenship should be based on annual activity reports,

letters of appreciation that go beyond the perfunctory thanks, and especially requests that an individual give repeat performances (No good deed goes unpunished!). The absence of evidence of *un*satisfactory citizenship should never be interpreted as satisfactory performance. Creative measures of the quality and quantity of such contributions would be helpful.

5. We recommend that programs formulate mission statements to guide the setting of faculty roles and the allocation of rewards among those who perform them. Much of the stress over faculty roles and rewards emanates from the absence of mission statements that would provide a coherent framework for evaluating faculty performance. When such mission statements exist, they often are not linked to faculty roles and rewards in ways that are obvious to faculty members, especially junior scholars. Faculty members deserve unambiguous statements of the missions of the institutions and programs in which they profess. They deserve accurate descriptions of the criteria that will be used to assess how much they contribute to those missions. They deserve criteria that have been formulated in ways that permit them to document the quality and the quantity of those contributions.

6. We recommend that definitions of faculty rewards be broadened beyond current formulations. Academic geographers earn external and internal rewards for fulfilling their roles well. External rewards may include:

   ▶ Job security in the form of long-term tenure.
   ▶ Promotion to higher academic ranks.
   ▶ Merit increases of base salaries.
   ▶ Temporary salary augmentations.
   ▶ Grants to underwrite research.
   ▶ Reimbursement for expenses of field work, travel, conference participation, and research materials.
   ▶ Working space and equipment.
   ▶ Student assistance.
   ▶ Prizes and awards.
   ▶ Public and peer recognition.

   Internal rewards may include personal satisfaction over role performance that yields an enhanced sense of self-worth and pride in accomplishment, unusual opportunities for self-reflection, freedom to redirect one's professional efforts, a high degree of professional autonomy, and abundant opportunities to contribute to community welfare by drawing on professional expertise. Faculty reward schemes in

American colleges and universities focus primarily on external awards for good reason — it is easier to obtain and allocate external awards than to cultivate the leadership skills that arouse faculty members' internal motivations.

In an era when external rewards are likely to remain stagnant, it is worth reminding ourselves that effective leaders usually offer their followers few external rewards. On the contrary, their followers often make great personal sacrifices to enlist in powerful movements because they have been convinced that they will engage in a great cause that will ennoble their lives. The pursuit, transformation, and transmission of knowledge *is* a great cause. Individual faculty members, caught up in the whirlwinds of the many jobs they do, easily forget the larger enterprise in which they are engaged. Program and institutional leaders squander a powerful motivation and abdicate their responsibilities when they fail frequently to remind their faculty of the nobility of the roles they perform.

7. Finally, we recommend that academic administrators and faculty acknowledge that reward mechanisms now are based almost entirely on individualistic conceptions of faculty roles. Without exception in the committee's experience, rewards accrue to individuals evaluated in isolation. That view of faculty roles may prevail for some time. We opine, however, that the kinds of collaborative and team efforts that have proved productive in other industries eventually will prove useful in geography, probably in the form of instructional teams using several complementary methods of instruction. Research in geography also may move beyond the artisan or craft scale that currently prevails to projects that are addressed by organized groups.

Different individuals make different kinds of contributions to the success of a program. Excellent teaching and advising, outstanding research, intensive outreach, and heroic citizenship rarely are embodied in the same individuals. Therefore, the corporate success of most programs depends on individual faculty contributing more to some roles than to others. Reward systems that respond to that reality engender better relationships among colleagues and foster the achievement of collective program goals. We believe that thinking about ways to define roles and allocate rewards on a supra-individual basis deserves consideration as part of the general, long-term rethinking of reward schemes.

RECOMMENDATIONS ARE NOT PRESCRIPTIONS

In preparing these recommendations, we debated a variety of ways of conceptualizing faculty roles and rewards, including those used across a spectrum of academic institutions. We drew upon the customs, procedures, and practices used in determining faculty roles and rewards in specialties as different as chemistry and fine arts. We sought to cast these recommendations in a framework that is generic enough to be used, with local modifications, in almost any academic institution. We are confident that these recommendations are well founded in the experience and thinking of the wide range of institutions and disciplines we reviewed, but we stress the need to tailor their implementation to local expectations regarding faculty roles and appropriate rewards.

Institutional missions vary greatly among American colleges and universities, and program missions differ considerably, not only among institutions, but also within them. A geography program in a university whose primary mission is research may choose to concentrate on teaching and outreach. Alternatively, a geography program in an avowedly teaching institution may develop exceptional research expertise, and the institution's officers may elect to protect and enhance that role for its intrinsic and extrinsic value. A role and reward structure that fails to accommodate such local conditions is unlikely to yield satisfying results.

These recommendations will be helpful, therefore, only as they are tailored to what institutions and constituent units need to do and to the expertise and preferences of the faculty members who must meet those needs. Specificity in applying these recommendations should be carried well beyond program levels. Negotiated modifications of these general principles that suit individual faculty members, and indeed the several stages that occur in an individual's career cycle, should be expected and welcome. Failure to seek and find appropriate specificity will increase the risk of substituting new and different mismatches between faculty and institutional expectations for the traditional mismatches we hope to remedy. □

American Chemical Society

REPORT OF THE AMERICAN CHEMICAL SOCIETY TASK FORCE ON THE DEFINITION OF SCHOLARSHIP IN CHEMISTRY*

J. Ivan Legg, Memphis State University, *Co-Chair*; Laurence A. Nafie, Syracuse University, *Co-Chair*; Paula P. Brownlee, Association of American Colleges; William E. Broderick, State University of New York, Albany; Norman C. Craig, Oberlin College; Marcetta Y. Darensbourg, Texas A&M University; William B. DeLauder, Delaware State College; Slayton A. Evans, Jr., University of North Carolina; Ursula M. Mazur, Washington State University; Theodore E. Tabor, The Dow Chemical Company; Edward K. Mellon, Florida State University; Joseph G. Morse, Utah State University.

INTRODUCTION

This report is the result of deliberations of a special task force of the American Chemical Society to consider the definition of scholarship in the discipline of chemistry. The motivation to form the task force stems from a larger project being conducted by Syracuse University with grants from the Lilly Endowment and the Fund for the Improvement of Postsecondary Education to develop a wide range of discipline-specific definitions of scholarship and scholarly work. The goal of the Syracuse project, in light of changes and forces at work in higher education today, is to recognize a wider range of faculty activity, on a discipline-by-discipline basis, as scholarly activity. These forces, some financial, some political, some social, are calling for institutions of higher education to be more responsive to their roles of teaching students and providing various kinds of community service. The traditional way of categorizing faculty activity as teaching, research, and service, with research holding an elevated position of importance relative to teaching and service, is not fully supportive of the changes that are occurring and need to occur. The goal of this report is to provide a more general and flexible definition of scholarship in chemistry that can be tailored to the needs of individual institutions, academic, industrial or governmental, that generate or evaluate scholarly work in chemistry.

---

* Reprinted with the permission of the American Chemical Society.

TRADITIONAL SCHOLARSHIP

For the past several decades the paradigm for scholarship in chemistry has been research. The words scholarship and research have become nearly synonymous in referring to the discovery of new knowledge about molecules and chemical systems, the publication of research papers, reviews and monographs, the writing of grant proposals, the management of funded research projects, the contribution to scientific meetings and the training of graduate students and postdoctoral associates. Faculty activities in the areas of undergraduate teaching and service, particularly at research universities, has been regarded as necessary and sometimes important but of a distinctly lower stature and fundamental significance. This value system has led to an atmosphere of competition between chemistry departments in which each department has as its fundamental goal to move into the tier of chemistry departments ranked just above it in prestige and research excellence.

While such goals are laudable and an important part of the extremely high standards, on a world-wide basis, achieved by chemistry departments in the United States, these goals are not sensitive to the adverse conditions presently confronting institutions of higher education, as well as the discipline of chemistry as a whole. Today, chemists are faced, more than ever, with the need to be accountable to state legislatures that fund public institutions, to students and their parents who pay high tuition fees at private universities, to the general public which does not understand the science of chemistry or what happens in institutions of higher education, and to the quality of our pre-college (K-12) educational system which has the task of preparing the minds of the chemistry scholars of tomorrow.

At the department level, the traditional definition of scholarship in chemistry has led to the occurrence of some faculty dissatisfaction, low morale, and lost potential. The headlong pursuit of research excellence has led to a departmental social structure that depresses the stature of faculty members who are not very productive in research. These faculty members in some instances are regarded as second class citizens or deadwood, and often feel no motivation to contribute strongly to the overall activity of the department. In these changing times, an important source of faculty energy for carrying out projects of importance to the department, such as curriculum revision or public outreach, is these under-utilized faculty members.

GENERALIZED SCHOLARSHIP

In order to provide a basis for responding to the changing needs of chemistry as a discipline, we offer a definition of scholarship in chemistry that is broader and more general than the traditional definition of chemistry scholarship. This definition recognizes that scholarship as an activity can occur in many different forms in many different areas of human intellectual activity. Most fundamentally, scholarship can be viewed as a process of reasoning, reflection, integration or communication that leads to new knowledge, insights, methods or modes of thought. For a particular discipline, such as chemistry, there are many different products of scholarship, as well as degrees of scholarship in various kinds of activities.

The general definition of scholarship that we support involves thinking about scholarship in two dimensions. Along one dimension are the different areas of activity in which elements of scholarship can be found. These areas are listed without reference to intrinsic relative importance. It is left to the institutions, departments or organizational units that implement this definition to specify the relative importance to be placed on the various areas. In this way the definition is flexible and adaptable to all kinds of settings in which scholarship in chemistry occurs. The second dimension of the generalized definition of scholarship is a set of criteria that vary along a continuum from the highest degree to the lowest degree for the evaluation of the quality or degree of scholarship in any of the scholarship areas along the first dimension.

We have selected four basic areas along the first dimension in which chemistry scholarship can occur, and within each area we list examples of more specific activities. The examples are meant to be illustrative, and not comprehensive, of the types of activity in that area. These basic areas are:

Scholarship Areas:

Research	Application	Teaching	Outreach
▶ Discovery	▶ Industrial	▶ Classroom preparation	▶ Scientific literacy
▶ Integration	▶ Reduction to practice	▶ Curriculum development	▶ K-12 enrichment
▶ Publications	▶ Technology transfer	▶ Graduate students	▶ Extension service
▶ Grants		▶ Textbooks	▶ Ethics
▶ Monographs		▶ Multimedia materials	▶ Minority/gender recruitment

For a given area, or a specific activity in that area, the importance of the scholarship can be evaluated along the second dimension using a single set of criteria according to the following list:

Scholarship Criteria:
Degree or extent of:
▶ Recognition
— awards
— invited papers and colloquia
▶ Communication with colleagues or peers
— publications
— books or monographs
▶ Financial support
— external or institutional grants

At the highest level of scholarship in a given area there is fame and international recognition, a prolific degree of publication in the most respected journals, and a high degree of grant support. At the lowest level there is little or no recognition outside the immediate activity, there is no communication with peers, and no financial support. It is possible, at least in principle, to reach the highest level of scholarship in any of the four areas listed, although it is most common to do so in the area of research.

The task force feels that research enjoys a unique status with respect to the areas of application, teaching, and outreach, listed above. Of these four areas, research is the only one that consists entirely of scholarship. One cannot carry out research without being involved in scholarly activity. On the other hand, for the other areas, there is often a significant component of the activity which is not scholarship. These non-scholarship components are usually activities that support or promote scholarship and are vital to the sustenance of excellent scholarship.

IMPORTANCE OF SCHOLARSHIP

Scholarship represents the highest level of intellectual activity in the various areas of chemistry. It corresponds to those elements of activity that are new, thought-provoking, interactive, long-lasting and transportable between individuals or organizational units. Scholarship at the highest levels is what we all strive to achieve.

The task force believes that involvement in research in the present or recent past is necessary to achieve excellence in performance and high levels of scholarship in the other areas outlined above. This is particularly true in the area of teaching where it is often observed that outstanding teachers are active and enthusiastic researchers. There is a strong interplay between teaching and research which is vital to the former. Chemistry is a discipline where discoveries and new concepts of a fundamental nature are continually coming to light. To stay current as a teacher, and to appreciate the limits of established principles, one should have had direct experience with the research process and the scientific method. Outstanding teaching involves reaching beyond the bounds of standardized textbook material in a scholarly manner to expose the students to new developments in chemistry. This requires extra effort of a reflective and reasoned manner that goes beyond the mere presentation of facts for learning by students.

By extending the definition of scholarship beyond the area of research, the task force does not want to downplay the importance of research to the discipline of chemistry. Rather, we seek to encourage individuals who are so inclined to carry out scholarship in other areas besides research, and thereby contribute in a valuable way to the development, strength, and changing nature of the field of chemistry. This encouragement will become effective when individuals, from the practicing chemist to the highest levels of administration or management, recognize and reward other forms of chemistry scholarship. We hope to promote the simple idea that research is not the only quality game in town. We feel that acceptance of this idea will benefit the discipline of chemistry as a whole.

DISCUSSION

The fundamental conclusion of this report is that scholarship takes place in a wide variety of activities related to the discipline of chemistry, and we have provided a framework for identifying and evaluating the significance of these various forms of scholarship. Within this framework, we conclude that although research is only scholarship, not all scholarship is research. We believe that the traditional division of faculty performance into the categories of teaching, research, and service, is still useful and valid, provided that it is recognized that scholarship can also occur in the areas of teaching and [service]. In choosing the areas in which scholarship occurs we have followed ideas in the writings of Ernest Boyer and others that subdivide forms of scholarship into the scholarship of discovery, the scholarship of integration, the scholarship of application and the scholarship of teaching. In adapting this framework to the discipline of chemistry we have combined the scholarships of discovery and integration of knowledge into research, and we have added a new area that we refer to as the scholarship of outreach.

For illustrative purposes we present a few examples of scholarship outside the traditional area of research. In the case of teaching, scholarship can take the form of writing a textbook, developing a new approach to teaching a particular chemical concept, or developing a new experiment for a laboratory exercise or a novel lecture demonstration. In the examples of curricular development, an important component of the scholarly activity is the publication or the dissemination of the results of the development. Similarly, in the case of community outreach, the creation of new approaches to stimulating the interest of elementary school children in careers in science and the communication of such insights through books, monographs, reports or publications represent an important form of scholarship. Interest in the area of outreach as an area of vital importance to the discipline of chemistry is relatively new and undeveloped. As such, the number of avenues available for the expression of scholarship is more limited than that for research, but more opportunities should arise in the future as more effort in this area is expended.

Although the definition of scholarship adopted by the task force is general, there are several areas associated with scholarship in chemistry that are discipline-specific. One is the considerable expense of carrying out research at the highest levels of excellence and innovation. Only a relatively select group of institutions have the financial resources to maintain truly first-rate chemistry faculty and research programs. Another area is the close relation between teaching and research discussed in some detail above. Not all disciplines are changing as rapidly as chemistry at the level of introductory courses, and as a consequence the accurate and relevant introduction of this subject to students requires a person in tune with current events in important areas of chemistry, one who appreciates the nature of research in chemistry. A particular problem that arises in the teaching of introductory chemistry is what to teach. If new material is simply appended to existing material, the depth of the course is reduced leaving only short statements of fact rather than thoughtful, instructive subject areas. Clearly, there is ample opportunity for creative scholarship in the design of new textbooks and course curricula under these dynamic circumstances.

Another impression that the task force does not want to emerge from this report is the notion that activities that do not fall into the category of scholarship are not important. There are many types of activity in the areas of application, teaching, and research that will be on the border between scholarship and non-scholarship, between the reasoned, reflective activity leading to communication of methods and ideas to others and the simple act of just working out the details of an application, grading exam questions or performing some form of outreach activity. All of these activities are important to the overall mission of chemistry, and it is far less important to worry about what things are called than it is to recognize and nurture important activities. Organizational units should find ways to encourage a wider range of individual contribution so that the goals of that unit can be approached more rapidly and effectively.

CONCLUSIONS

In this report we have recommended an extension of the traditional definition of scholarship in chemistry. The new definition is general and can be adapted to a wide range of organizational units in academics, industry or government by specifying the relative importance of the various areas presented, or even adding new ones as desired. The report stresses the importance of scholarship in chemistry but also recognizes the importance of non-scholarship activities that are directly or indirectly supportive of scholarship. It is hoped that the expanded definition of scholarship will foster a more complete and efficient utilization of individuals in organizational units, a utilization in which a wider range of talents is brought to bear on important issues to chemistry in these times of change, growth, and adaptation. □

Joint Policy Board for Mathematics

RECOGNITION AND REWARDS IN THE MATHEMATICAL SCIENCES*

Report of the Joint Policy Board for Mathematics, Committee on Professional Recognition and Rewards *(excerpt)*

RECOMMENDATION AND GUIDING PRINCIPLES

After reflecting on its study and findings, the Committee discussed at some length a wide variety of possible recommendations. We came to the conclusion that, given the enormous diversity of institutions of higher education and departments, only one general recommendation could be made:

The recognition and rewards system in the mathematical sciences departments must encompass the full array of faculty activity required to fulfill departmental and institutional missions.

We learned from our study of the rewards structure that this perhaps self-evident recommendation is being implemented in only a small number of departments, and only a somewhat larger number are even beginning to grapple with the issues it entails. There is a clear need for departments to implement the changes that are required to achieve the goal stated in the recommendation. To this end, we offer the following six Guiding Principles to assist faculty and chairs.

GUIDING PRINCIPLE I

Research in the mathematical sciences and its applications is fundamental to the existence and utility of the discipline and should continue to be among the primary factors of importance in the recognition and rewards system.

Discussion

The accomplishments in mathematical research in the last twenty-five years have been truly remarkable. Numerous new branches of the subject have developed, while seemingly rigid boundaries between subfields have given way to robust cross-fertilization. The merging of what earlier were considered distinct fields has contributed to the solution of a number of famous, longstanding problems in core mathematics. Similarly, major breakthroughs have been made in various fields of applied mathematics. Moreover, core and applied mathematics have continued to enrich one another. In addition, mathematical methods and constructs are increasingly important in science, engineering, business, and industry, and problems arising from these sources are enriching the field.

The mathematical sciences must be internally strong. It also must have lively connections to other disciplines and to business and industry. Otherwise, many activities of the mathematical sciences community — such as teaching mathematics, curriculum development, expository writing, research in mathematics education, and many others — would lose the basis on which they rest. Research must therefore continue to be among the most important components of the rewards system.

The Committee believes that no distinction should be made in the rewards system between research in the core areas of mathematics and that in applied areas. For example, much research in computational and applied mathematics is essentially the same as research in traditional mathematics, with both centering on the construction of new theory. However, these nontraditional areas are characterized by activities that are unusual in traditional mathematics departments, such as interdisciplinary research leading to publications with numerous authors, numerical experimentation that is not documented in traditional journals, and development of large computer codes that take years to complete, that are used primarily for simulation studies and/or design decisions, and that often have nontraditional methods of dissemination. The rewards structure needs to be sensitive to these differences.

Interdisciplinary research (such as mathematics in materials science, mathematics in biology, mathematics in environment sciences, mathematics in industry, to name a few areas) requires a large investment of time and effort in learning new subjects and in developing a project before any results can be achieved. Departments that wish to encourage interdisciplinary research must recognize these difficulties and adapt the rewards system accordingly. We believe that, for interdisciplinary research to thrive, there must be a means for making joint appointments with other departments, with joint evaluations. This can be a thorny issue, since universities tend to be sharply organized along departmental lines. The central administration, deans, and chancellors can play a constructive role here.

GUIDING PRINCIPLE II

Each department should ensure that contributions to teaching and related activities and to service are among the primary factors of importance in the recognition and rewards system.

Discussion

Different departments place different amounts of emphasis on research, depending on the departmental and institutional missions. In all departments, however, the teaching function should be viewed as a primary responsibility of all faculty and should be rewarded and recognized accordingly. Teaching the next generation of those who need to use mathematics is not only one of the most fulfilling activities of a faculty member, it is also fundamental to the existence of the discipline. This responsibility extends far beyond the professor's time in the classroom to include curriculum development, advising, contributing to the training of graduate students, and other instructional activities.

For example, revitalizing and reforming undergraduate mathematics education is one of the principal challenges facing the profession today. Much of great value has already been accomplished and there is a marked increase in faculty interest in and excitement about these issues. The wide availability of the computer and the growing awareness of the opportunities for innovation that it provides add to the interest and excitement. Departments should encourage experiments in teaching and see to it that no unnecessary obstacles are placed in the way of innovative or nontraditional approaches. In addition, departments should communicate the importance of teaching by making formal efforts to help faculty and graduate students improve their teaching. This can be done by having those who are acknowledged to be superb teachers help others improve, or by calling upon campus resources (such as centers for teaching).

Two-year colleges have an especially long history of interest in and experience with successful teaching, especially with teaching underprepared students. Increasing numbers of students start their mathematics education at two-year schools and later transfer to baccalaureate institutions. For these reasons, we encourage more cooperation between two- and four-year schools through transfer agreements and joint course planning.

Departments and institutions cannot survive without faculty who are willing to take on substantial service responsibilities. These include chairing the department, managing the undergraduate or graduate programs, managing the advising program, serving on departmental and institutional committees, preparing graduate students for the realities of the jobs they will fill inside and outside academia, recruiting and mentoring minority and women students and scholars, and assuming leadership roles based on professional expertise in the local community, and especially in the K-12 schools, or in professional organizations. These duties — all of them essential to the health and well-being of the institution and to mathematics in general — should be valued as important components of the recognition and rewards system.

GUIDING PRINCIPLE III

Departments should develop policies that encourage faculty to allocate their efforts in ways that are as consistent as possible with their current interests and, at the same time, fit the needs of the department. The goal should be to create a department that meets all its obligations and aspirations with excellence, while at the same time engaging faculty in activities that they find personally rewarding. These activities should be recognized as valuable, and they should be rewarded when done well.

Discussion

The various duties of a department should be seen as a shared or corporate responsibility of the entire department. These duties include teaching, scholarship, advising, curriculum development, faculty development, mentoring young faculty, recruitment, service to the institution, and working to increase the diversity of the undergraduate and graduate student body. Moreover, all departments must accept responsibility for helping to increase mathematical literacy in American society. Indeed, the health of the nation is threatened by the fact that large groups of our population have traditionally remained, and continue to remain, unconversant with science, engineering, mathematics, and technology. Depending on the institutional and departmental missions, these responsibilities may also include research, mentoring of doctoral students, articulation between high school and college, outreach, service to the community and to the nation, involvement with K-12 education, and liaison with industry.

The optimal strategy for meeting these varied departmental responsibilities is not to expect all faculty members in the department to do all things at all times, but rather to match faculty work with faculty interests so that, to the extent possible, each faculty member accepting a departmental duty has an interest in that duty and will perform it well. For example, a faculty member who needs extra time for research may be freed from student advising because another faculty member prefers to focus on advising. This can result in a net gain for the department in both research productivity and quality of advising, as well as a higher level of satisfaction for both faculty members. But, in order to work, this approach must be accompanied by a rewards system that recognizes excellent contributions to all facets of the departmental mission. In order to recognize the shared responsibility for fulfilling the mission of the department, some rewards might productively be restructured as group or department rewards.

It should not be assumed that faculty members will throughout their careers continue to have the same interests and the same ways of contributing to their departments and profession. Departmental planning should take account of these changing interests, and the rewards structure should be flexible enough to recognize that the kinds of contributions that a given faculty member makes may vary over time. At the same time, departments need to state clearly what they are about and must appropriately support the expectations that they lay out. This is especially important with junior, untenured faculty. For instance, to a considerable extent everyone should be involved in research or scholarship, allowing for (sometimes large) differences according to institutions, in the expected level of achievement. Departments wishing to have their members actively engaged in research certainly need to encourage and support their members in this activity, and under these conditions research would become a relatively large factor in hiring and tenure decisions.

We encourage regular consultations between chairs and individual faculty members about the needs of the department, the goals of the faculty members, and the best match between the two. Such consultations would provide one way to enhance communication and address the problems described in Finding V. These consultations should include discussion of the scholarly, teaching, and service interests of the faculty and should result in agreements on how faculty members will allocate their time and effort over the next year or two. The rewards system should then support these agreements.

In addition, we encourage the use of periodic reviews for all faculty members, tenured as well as untenured. Spaced at intervals of perhaps three to five years, these reviews are important for optimizing the effective use of the department's personnel and for identifying areas that need attention or that merit special recognition. Such reviews will also help address the problem of declining public confidence in higher education.

Finally, one of the most important functions of a department is the development of the talent of its junior faculty. Such mentoring could include helping these faculty members keep abreast of the current situation in the job market and how best to be successful in it, know how well they are progressing toward the goal of a permanent position, keep informed of the requirements for tenure if they have tenure-track positions, and begin a viable research and teaching career. We encourage departments to put into place a system in which mentoring is a well-defined responsibility of the senior faculty and one for which they are recognized and rewarded. Such a system would also help to ameliorate the communication problems described in Finding V as well as help to ensure the future well-being of the department.

GUIDING PRINCIPLE IV

All faculty members in colleges and universities should engage in scholarship throughout their careers and the institution and department should encourage, support, and reward this activity. Moreover, each department, together with the institution, should develop a working definition of scholarship that is consistent with the departmental and institutional missions and is sufficiently encompassing and flexible to embrace the broad variety of intellectual activities in the discipline.

Discussion

The mathematical sciences as a discipline is held together by the glue of research and scholarship. The fundamental role of research has been discussed in Guiding Principle I. The many and varied activities that come under the more general umbrella of scholarship are also of critical importance to the mathematical sciences. These activities include, but are not limited to, writing expository papers and textbooks, communicating mathematical developments to the general public, developing curricula, improving teaching methods, and research in mathematics education.

This kind of intellectual activity is crucial to teaching effectiveness. A teacher must be intellectually alive in a discipline to be able to communicate the subject effectively to students, regardless of the level of the teaching. Therefore, with appropriate modifications in the definition of scholarship, this Principle applies to all institutions of higher education.

A proposal for a definition of scholarship appears in the Appendix of this report. Of course, a single definition of scholarship cannot be appropriate for every institution and department. Each department should interpret this definition according to its mission, the mission of its institution, and the needs of its constituents. Our purpose in presenting this definition of scholarship is to start a dialogue, not to dictate a definition for all institutions. In addition, the amount of scholarship expected from faculty members should be consistent with the amount of assigned teaching and other duties at the institution.

Every department has a sufficiently broad scope of responsibilities to allow a great deal of flexibility in its definition of scholarship. For example, the scholarly activities of a given individual should be allowed to vary over that individual's career. At the beginning of a career, especially at a research university, scholarship might consist principally of traditional research. But some senior faculty might be encouraged and rewarded in efforts to pursue other forms of scholarship.

GUIDING PRINCIPLE V

Evaluation goes hand in hand with rewards. Departments should use the best available methods, imperfect though they may be, for evaluating teaching, research, scholarship, and service while also seeking to develop better methods of evaluation. Meanwhile, discomfort with current methods of evaluation is no reason not to reward the full range of professorial contributions.

Discussion

Every institution should work to develop efficient, robust, reliable, and trusted measures of teaching effectiveness. These could include peer evaluation, surveying of students from previous semesters (say, graduating seniors or alumni), studying student achievement in subsequent courses, reviewing syllabi and examinations, and other techniques. The perceived inability to evaluate teaching is one of the major stumbling blocks to making teaching an integral part of the rewards system in mathematical sciences departments. It is critical that this perception be changed. In addition, departments should develop evaluation mechanisms for such teaching-related activities as curriculum development, administering the teaching program, advising and mentoring students, and outreach to minorities and women.

By far the most common (and often the only) method of evaluating teaching is the student evaluation form. Many faculty members feel that, when used as the sole measure of teaching effectiveness, student evaluations can be misleading and unreliable. The Committee agrees, but also believes that student evaluations, when collected over many semesters and over a number of courses, can identify important issues that faculty members and department chairs need to consider.

Methods should also be developed to evaluate scholarship that does not fit into the traditional mode of publishing in refereed journals. Much mathematical work that could be valuable is discouraged because it is not sufficiently rewarded. The important aspects of research are that it be shared with the community and that it be of high quality.

Service — whether to the department, the institution, the mathematical sciences community, or the nation — is often said to be the most difficult work to evaluate. However, because service is critical to departments, institutions, and the profession, appropriate mechanisms must be formulated to evaluate it. We note that the performance of the department chair is constantly evaluated formally from above and informally from below.

Departments also need to develop procedures for documenting and evaluating the overall performance and contributions of faculty members. This is not only needed to be able to reward faculty members for their contributions, but also to provide useful feedback for the faculty. Usually, much more is known about the performance of the individuals in the department than is acknowledged. Each faculty member needs to know that contributions which further the departmental and institutional missions and are of sufficiently high quality will be valued and rewarded.

A common method of evaluating faculty is on the basis of receipt of grants from outside the university. These could be grants for either mathematical research or mathematics education projects. The "best" grants are often considered to be those with the largest overhead rate. We found tremendous unhappiness among faculty concerning excessive reliance on grant awards in the rewards system. As one faculty member put it, departments have switched from "publish or perish" to "get grants or go." There is clearly some validity to rewarding individuals whose work is judged to be of sufficiently high merit to warrant such funding. However, the amount of money available is so small that even excellent work is often not funded. Also, many of the contributions faculty members make are not "fundable". It is a serious mistake to let external funding control the rewards structure.

Departments should not allow imperfections in evaluation mechanisms to impede progress in broadening the rewards structure. After all, such problems have not hampered the use of traditional research published in refereed journals as a primary component of the rewards structure. One of the reasons research is singled out in this way is that most people feel comfortable evaluating it. The fact that outside evaluators (the editor and the referee) have given their blessing to a work by publishing it constitutes an objective criterion one can point to. On the other hand, we found considerable suspicion in the community about the objectivity of this criterion. Moreover, for most faculty, an in-depth formal analysis of research quality is done only two or three times, at hiring and promotion. The annual research review is often much more cursory, perhaps only involving a listing of articles. Still, these imperfections in evaluating research have been no impediment to its important role in the rewards structure.

National leadership on the issue of evaluation is needed. For example, a task force could be set up by the professional societies in the mathematical sciences to assess the evaluation systems currently being used and to create guidelines, models or suggestions for helping institutions improve their evaluation procedures. A compilation of the procedures that are already in use would also be a service. Other organizations in academia are examining such questions. For example, the American Association for Higher Education is studying the method of peer evaluation of teaching. Such studies should be examined for their applicability to mathematical sciences departments.

There have been many studies on the efficacy of student evaluations of teaching. We urge the professional societies to review this body of research as it relates to the teaching of mathematics. Also, there should be further research into various measures of teaching effectiveness, taking into account the special nature of mathematics teaching and the students, many of whom must take mathematics courses to fulfill university or major requirements. Such research would provide background for formulating guidelines, models, and recommendations for evaluating teaching.

GUIDING PRINCIPLE VI

Each department should ensure that its rewards structure is responsive to meeting the needs of the constituencies being served. An essential aspect of any well-functioning rewards structure is that all concerned — faculty, chair, and administration — know and understand what is valued and rewarded.

Discussion

No single rewards system will work for every mathematical sciences department in every kind of institution. Each department must develop a rewards system consonant with its own mission and the mission of the institution. In formulating a rewards structure, each department must analyze who its constituencies are, what they need from the department, and whether those needs are being met. The constituencies of a department are varied and many, and often not all of them are adequately taken into account in how the department organizes itself, designs and provides its services, and utilizes its resources.

To varying degrees, depending on the institution, these constituencies include: undergraduate students and graduate students, both inside and outside the department; colleagues in other departments; mathematical colleagues; parents of students; local, state, and national government; taxpayers; the regional and national community; and business and industry. The point is that the rewards structure should be responsive to meeting the needs of these constituencies.

At the same time, the nature of academia is such that not everyone fits into the same mold, and this must be acknowledged and understood. Therefore, rather than codifying every aspect of a rewards system, departments should formulate clear and flexible policies.

The department chair is the leader in the implementation of any rewards system. Care in the selection and training of the chair is an important factor in the health and well-being of the department. Too little attention is paid to this important role. Every department should carefully select, and then support, a chair who understands the issues facing the department and who can deal with the multiple agendas in the institution. The mathematical sciences community can help by organizing more workshops for chairs and other training and development mechanisms.

CONCLUDING REMARKS

We urge that departments move forward on the recommendation and agenda presented in this report. We also urge the professional societies to move forward on studies of some of the specific issues raised in this report. Above all, we urge that the mathematical sciences community continue, and indeed expand, the dialogue that has already begun on these important issues. It is only from thoughtful, considered discussion and debate that lasting change will emerge.

APPENDIX

Defining Mathematical Scholarship

College and university faculty members are scholars as well as teachers. They must stay abreast of the latest developments in their fields in order to remain effective as teachers. Society looks to academia to advance the frontiers of knowledge and to communicate those advances not only to their students but also to the larger public. Colleges and universities provide a particularly supportive environment for free inquiry, discovery, and the incubation of ideas. Academic scholars provide an important resource that can be drawn upon to address pressing local, regional, and national needs.

But what is scholarship? For some, scholarship is defined narrowly as research leading to new knowledge that is publishable in the leading research journals. Others define scholarship broadly as any activity that leads to increased knowledge or understanding on the part of the individual scholar. Between these two extremes is a variety of activities that may or may not be recognized as scholarly by those who make judgements about scholarship: deans, department chairs, colleagues and students, journal editors, and the public.

Each mathematical sciences department should formulate an explicit and public definition of scholarship that will inform its faculty members on the kinds of scholarly activity that are valued by the department, guide administrators and review committees that are charged with evaluating and rewarding that scholarship, and help all interested parties to understand the scholarly component of the departmental mission. This definition should, of course, be consistent with the mission of the institution. It should embrace the variety of scholarly activities in all fields that the institution and the department wish to encourage and support.

Following is a draft definition of scholarship for the mathematical sciences that may serve as a guide to departments seeking to formulate their own definitions. This draft will, of course, need to be modified by each department to reflect its own values and mission and to conform to the institutional mission.

Scholarship in the mathematical sciences includes:

▶ research in core or applied areas that leads to new concepts, insights, discoveries, structures, theorems, or conjectures;

▶ research that leads to the development of new mathematical techniques, or new applications of known techniques, for addressing problems in other fields including the sciences, the social sciences, medicine and engineering;

▶ research in teaching and learning that leads to new insights into how mathematical knowledge and skills are most effectively taught and learned at all levels;

▶ synthesis, or integration, of existing scholarship, such as surveys, book reviews, and lists of open problems;

▶ exposition that communicates mathematics to new audiences, or to established audiences with improved clarity, either orally or in writing, including technical communications to scientists, engineers, and other mathematicians, as well as books, articles, multimedia materials, and presentations for teachers, government leaders, and the general public;

▶ development of courses, curricula, or instructional materials for teaching mathematics in K-12 as well as at the college level; and

▶ development of software that provides new or improved tools for supporting research in mathematics or its applications, for communicating mathematics, or for teaching and learning mathematics.

Good scholarship, in whatever form it takes, must be shared in order to have value. It must benefit more than just the scholar. The results of scholarly activities must be public and must be amenable to evaluation. Techniques appropriate for the evaluation of scholarship in the mathematical sciences include peer review and invitations to present results to others; awards and other forms of recognition; and impact measures, such as citations, evidence of the use of the scholarship in the work of others, evidence of improved effectiveness of a technique or activity as a result of the scholarly contribution, or evidence of improved understanding of mathematics on the part of some consumer group as a result of the scholarly activity.

BIBLIOGRAPHY

[1] Alpert, Daniel. "Rethinking the Challenges Facing the American Research University." Unpublished manuscript, Center for Advanced Study, University of Illinois at Urbana-Champaign.

[2] Anderson, Erin, editor. *Campus Use of the Teaching Portfolio: 25 Profiles.* Washington, D.C.: American Association for Higher Education, 1993.

[3] Atkinson, Richard and Tuzin, Donald. "Equilibrium in the Research University," *Change,* May/June 1992, pp. 21-31.

[4] Board on Mathematical Sciences. "Mathematical Sciences, Technology, and Economic Competitiveness." National Research Council. Washington, D.C.: National Academy Press, 1991.

[5] Board on Mathematical Sciences. "Renewing US Mathematics: A Plan for the 1990s." National Research Council. Washington, D.C.: National Academy Press, 1990.

[6] Board on Mathematical Sciences. "Actions for Renewing U.S. Mathematical Sciences Departments." National Research Council. Washington, D.C.: BMS, 1990.

[7] Board on Mathematical Sciences and Mathematical Sciences Education Board. "Moving Beyond Myths: Revitalizing Undergraduate Mathematics." Washington, D.C.: National Academy Press, 1991.

[8] Bok, Derek. "Reclaiming the Public Trust," *Change,* July/August 1992, pp. 13-19.

[9] Boyer, Ernest L. *Scholarship Reconsidered: Priorities of the Professoriate.* Princeton, NJ: The Carnegie Foundation for the Advancement of Teaching, 1990.

[10] Cole, Jonathan R. "Dilemmas of Choice Facing Research Universities," *Daedalus,* Fall 1993, pp. 1-33.

[11] Diamond, Robert M. and Bronwyn E. Adam, editors. *Recognizing Faculty Work: Reward Systems for the Year 2000.* San Francisco, CA: Jossey-Bass, 1993.

[12] Edgerton, Russell. "The Reexamination of Faculty Priorities," *Change,* July/Aug 1993, pp. 10-25.

[13] Edgerton, Russell, Patricia Hutchings, and Kathleen Quinlan. *The Teaching Portfolio: Capturing the Scholarship in Teaching.* Washington, DC: American Association for Higher Education, 1991.

[14] Elman, Sandra E., and Sue Marx Smock. *Professional Service and Faculty Rewards: Toward an Integral Structure.* Washington, D.C., National Association of State Universities and Land-Grant Colleges, 1985.

[15] Fairweather, James S. "Faculty Rewards Reconsidered: The Nature of Tradeoffs," *Change,* July/August 1993, pp. 44-47.

[16] Gray, P. and Robert M. Diamond. "A National Study of Research Universities on the Balance between Research and Undergraduate Teaching." Syracuse, NY: Syracuse University Center for Instructional Development, 1992.

[17] Hutchings, Patricia. *Using Cases to Improve College Teaching: A Guide to More Reflective Practice.* Washington, DC: American Association for Higher Education, 1993.

[18] Lovett, Clara. "American Professors and Their Society," *Change,* July/August 1993, pp. 26-37.

[19] National Science Foundation. "America's Academic Future: A Report of the Presidential Young Investigator Colloquium on U.S. Engineering, Mathematics, and Science Education for the Year 2010 and Beyond." Washington, D.C.: NSF Publication 91-150, 1992.

[20] Scott, David K. and Susan M. Awbrey. "Transforming Scholarship," *Change,* July/August 1993, pp. 38-43.

[21] Steen, Lynn Arthur. "20 Questions That Deans Should Ask Their Mathematics Department." *AAHE Bulletin,* May 1992, pp. 3-6. □

THE WORK OF ARTS FACULTIES IN HIGHER EDUCATION*

Landscape Architectural Accreditation Board, National Architectural Accrediting Board, National Association of Schools of Art and Design, National Association of Schools of Dance, National Association of Schools of Music, National Association of Schools of Theatre. *Consultant:* University Film and Video Association

I. ABOUT THIS DOCUMENT

Origin

Work in the various arts disciplines has a vital role in higher education throughout the United States. As both higher education and the arts evolve, old challenges reformulate themselves, and new challenges arise. Increasingly, choices are made while contexts change rapidly. Over time, policies, procedures, and personnel decisions define the scope, depth, and effectiveness of each institution's endeavors. In this context, few decisions are as important as those made about faculty.

The centrality of faculty issues has caused groups representing various academic disciplines to participate in a national project to consider the elements of faculty work. Each disciplinary group agreed to define and present its own elements and to explain

---

* Reproduced with the permission of the National Office for Arts Accreditation in Higher Education.

Disclaimer: This text is analytical and consultative only. Although produced by organizations that accredit, *it is not a statement of accreditation standards, policies, or processes, and must not be referenced as such.* Official accreditation documents are available from the separate accreditation associations for architecture, art and design, dance, landscape architecture, music, and theatre.

Copies, Extracts, Discs: This document is not copyrighted. It may be reproduced in whole or in part in the interest of education and cultural development. Any organization or institution may reproduce the document in quantities sufficient for its own use, but not for sale. Notice of credit should appear on all copies. Institutions and organizations are invited to use extracts from this document to develop or revise their own statements regarding the work of arts faculties. *The Work of Arts Faculties in Higher Education* is available on diskette. Inquiries may be directed to the National Office for Arts Accrediting Associations whose telephone number and address are found elsewhere in this document.

To Contact Participating Organizations: *For Art and Design, Dance, Film/Video, Music, and Theatre:* National Office for Arts Accreditation in Higher Education, 11250 Roger Bacon Drive, Suite 21, Reston, VA 22090; Telephone 703-437-0700; Fax 703-437-6312 (the National Office will provide current information for contacting the University Film and Video Association.) *For Architecture:* National Architectural Accrediting Board, 1735 New York Avenue, N.W., Washington, DC 20006; Telephone 202-783-2007; Fax 202-626-7421. *For Landscape Architecture:* Landscape Architectural Accreditation Board, 4401 Connecticut Avenue, N.W., Fifth Floor, Washington, DC 20008-2302; Telephone 202-686-2752; Fax 202-686-1001.

their interrelationships in teaching, creative activity, research, and service. This document considers the arts in general and covers specifically the fields of architecture, art and design, dance, film and video, landscape architecture, music, and theatre. It is a consensus document completed after review by over one thousand programs in colleges, universities, and independent schools of the arts.

Purposes

Intellectual and creative powers are central to the work of all faculty. However, intellectual and creative activities, formats, and agendas can be employed for different purposes and to different effect both within and across disciplines. Our purposes are to explain the basic nature of intellectual and creative work in the arts and to present lists of responsibilities undertaken by arts faculties, thereby assisting development of local definitions and policies that support faculty work in the arts. We explain basic themes and premises, explore major analytical issues, annotate typical faculty activities, and provide advice about decision-making in institutional settings. Our analyses and recommendations are derived from the nature of work both *in* and *about* art. Our approach is intended to open possibilities for new thinking and new arrangements about the value of a broad range of activities that arts faculty undertake. We intend to encourage communication and understanding that assist local prioritization and evaluation.

Terminology

For purposes of this document, the term "arts" normally refers to all of the arts and arts-related disciplines and their subdisciplines. The term "unit" is used to designate the entire program in a particular arts discipline; thus, in specific cases, "unit" refers both to free-standing institutions and to departments or schools which are part of larger institutions.

"Making art" indicates the creation of an entirely new work of art or the creative process applied to performance. These activities may be mixed in a single effort, and they may be collaborative or individual. Our use of "making art" always indicates applications of knowledge, skills, and intellectual technique.

The word "work" is used in title and text because it provides an umbrella for the different types of faculty activities essential to the arts in higher education. This umbrella is necessary because definitions of such terms as creative activity, research, scholarship, teaching, and service can be narrow or broad. For example, when broadly defined, "research" can include the process of making a work of art: a search for the new is involved. When more narrow definitions based on science or humanities methodologies are applied, making art is not research, although research of scientific or humanistic types may be involved in the total art-making process. The word "work" enables respect and use of both narrow and broad definitions as institutions, organizations, and individuals may determine in specific circumstances. Whether broad or narrow, our use of "work" always indicates intense use of mind.

Standard descriptions of faculty work mention three areas. Two of these areas — teaching and service — seem to have common use throughout higher education. The third area, involving each faculty member's individual and collaborative work in one or more fields, is more problematic. Across the nation, various terminologies cover various concepts without much title/content consistency. The project task force struggled with this issue from numerous perspectives. As a result, the text uses "creative work and research" to name the third area. This formulation, while not perfect, has utility, especially if it is understood to express interrelationships rather than polarities. Creative work is an element of research; research is an element of creative work. Thus, making art and studying about art are both deeply intellectual. Our use of the word "intellectual" covers both of these activities.

II. FUNDAMENTALS

Mission, Goals, and Objectives

Definitions and policies concerning the work of the faculty are best developed and applied in terms of the specific mission, goals, and objectives present at each institution. Specific goals and objectives of various disciplinary programs may create a multiplicity of unique approaches and needs on a single campus. The following information and analysis should be used only in the contexts of and in relation to specific purposes, programs, and resources.

The Powers of Art

Works of art are powerful. They speak to, from, and through the emotions and the intellect. They reflect and stimulate passionate engagement. They provide cultural identity and engender civilization. But behind these powers lies the captivating force of aesthetic effect produced by organization, logic, and intellectual process. These attributes and conditions make the creation, interpretation, performance, and study of art central to higher education. It is the arts faculty, however, that provides the knowledge, skills, expertise, and long-term inspiration that keep the powers of art and our understandings about them at the highest possible levels.

The Arts as Disciplines

In some sense, all disciplines in higher education are concerned with discovering how things work, with what happened, with making new things, and with what things mean. Institutions, programs, the disciplines themselves, and their component activities arrange priorities for these concerns in different ways at different times, in accord with their various missions, goals, and objectives.

At base, the arts disciplines are all concerned with making new things. To make art is to compile a variety of elements into a unique arrangement. This happens every time a work of art is created or performed. But work in the arts disciplines goes much further. There are concerns with what happened, as revealed through the history of various art forms, with how things work in terms of internal mechanisms that generate artistic effectiveness, and with what things mean both in artistic and cultural terms and from other disciplinary perspectives. Over centuries, pursuit of these concerns has produced systematic, transmittable bodies of knowledge. The continued creation, discovery, storage, and transfer of this knowledge are the primary concerns of arts faculty.

Work *In* Art

Approaching the process of making art means approaching a realm that, whether simple or complex, is open-ended, often without empirical objectives, and frequently expressed in terms that are neither verbal nor mathematical. Creation, interpretation, and performance all involve communicating via the medium of an art form to produce a work. Each work, whether new or recreated, is a small universe of meaning with its own internal logics and mechanisms, whether standing alone or used in juxtaposition with other works, events, and functions. Each work also reflects and produces multiple universes of meaning as it relates to the external world where it is produced, received, and studied.

Work *About* Art

The study of art involves a vast complex of functions, purposes, and efforts. Each art form has its own history and body of analytical technique. Each has rich connections with general history and culture and with the analytical techniques of the sciences and the humanities. The "arts" as a group can be studied through disciplines ranging from aesthetics to management.

Critical Interrelationships

Taken as a whole, arts activities in higher education cover a broad range of work *in* and *about* art. Whatever objectives, definitions, and approaches are used, many critical interrelationships exist between the making and use of art on the one hand, and the study of completed work through research and scholarship on the other. Although the specifics of these interrelationships are defined and brought to bear in different ways to accomplish specific artistic, educational, and scholarly goals, the interrelationships themselves cannot be broken. Art-making processes, finished works of art, and research and scholarship about the arts and their impact are interdependent. Pursuit of any one creates some sort of relationship with the others.

Intellectual work involves creation, discovery, analysis, integration, synthesis, application, and evaluation. Weightings and arrangements of these elements vary across disciplines and across the activities, responsibilities, and perspectives associated with specific disciplines. In the arts, it is often a challenge to isolate and quantify these elements in analyses of faculty activities. Work in and about art, whether applied to teaching, individual activity in a field, or service, involves interrelationships among these elements that vary greatly within generic types of work. This is particularly true when creative activity, research, scholarship, teaching, and service are defined broadly.

Approaches and Perspectives

Making new things, considering what happened, discovering how things work, and searching for meaning become the basis for complex applications as individual institutions, faculties, and faculty members take various approaches to making art, studying art, and presenting art. When considering these approaches, it is important to make distinctions between media and methodologies. Each arts discipline can have its own mixtures of verbal, musical, visual, and kinesthetic media and its own sets of processes and techniques. Some processes and techniques are shared among the arts in general and some are discipline-specific. Specific works of art may combine the processes and techniques of two or more arts disciplines. And some art forms — architecture, landscape architecture, and design, for example — have close relationships with a variety of applied sciences.

Further, there are numerous perspectives for studying art. Singly or in combination, these perspectives can address how things work, what happened, what things mean, and can be used to gain competence in making new things. Several of the most common perspectives are:

▶ *Art as Process* — compilation, integration, and synthesis of (a) medium; (b) technical, historical, and analytical knowledge and skills; (c) inspiration and aspiration; and (d) ideas that result in a work of art.

▶ *Art as Product* — involvement with completed works presented, performed, or available for study from various perspectives; and the multiple interrelationships and influences of completed work.

▶ *Art as an Educative Force* — development of knowledge and skills in the arts, including mental and physical discipline gained from the study of art as process; and historical-cultural understanding gained from the study of completed work.

▶ *Art as Communication* — use of arts media and techniques to convey ideas and information for various purposes.

▶ *Art as a Psychological Phenomenon* — the impact of arts media on human behavior.

▶ *Art as a Physiological Phenomenon* — the impact of arts media on the human body.

▶ *Art as Therapeutics* — applications ranging from entertainment to psychology and psychiatry.

▶ *Art as Social Expression* — correlations of artistic modes, products, and perceptions with specific groups.

▶ *Art as Heritage* — correlations of artistic activity with cultures and times.

▶ *Art as Subject Matter for Other Disciplines* — use of points of view, methodologies, and contexts of the humanities, sciences, and social sciences to consider the impacts of art processes and products on intellectual, social, political, and other developments.

Intensive work involving these and other perspectives can be found throughout higher education. However, combinations, patterns, and emphases vary widely as various perspectives are mixed and balanced to achieve the goals and objectives of specific courses, curricula, institutions, and individual faculty projects.

Invention and Authenticity

Creative accomplishment for the artist means generating something that did not exist before. This is true whether the work is new, derivative, or interpretive. However, both newness and uniqueness are relative. While newness and uniqueness in and of themselves may be valid goals, much art-making involves work within aesthetic, temporal, or spatial limits. These may be determined by the artist or imposed by external conditions: use of the product; the specifics and structures of choreography, scores, and scripts; the availability of resources; the wishes of clients; intellectual climates; available technologies; and so forth. Authentic work by artist faculty thus ranges from experimentation that produces radical departures to applications of originality in a variety of standard formats.

Simplicity and Complexity

Faculty in all disciplines are expected to work as experts with complex issues and problems. Although artist faculty are no exception, a perceptual difficulty must be noted: the complexities of a work of art may not be readily apparent. The immediate impression may be one of naturalness and simplicity, but this effect may be achieved through complex techniques and structures that synthesize, integrate, and order multiple aesthetic elements. Studying art is usually quite different. Often, the goal is to reveal how things work, what happened and to what effect, and how meaning is evolving. Those considering the work of arts faculties in higher education need to understand the significance and validity of these multiple approaches. Surface simplicity can produce illusions that deny the presence of background complexity. While surface simplicity can produce immediate appeal — the music of Mozart, for example — it is the background complexities that provide the substance for intellectual analysis from an artistic perspective. When dealing comprehensively with matters of art, it is essential to remember that tremendous intellectual effort is involved both in hiding complexity and revealing it. Two further points are essential. First, simplicity *per se* (without underlying complexity) is a valid and laudable aesthetic goal, especially in certain artistic styles. Second, scholarly analysis that uncovers simple principles guiding either complex or simple art works can have all the attributes of analysis that uncovers underlying complexities.

Collaboration

Most visible in the performing arts, collaboration is present and growing in all arts disciplines. In collaborative situations, the individual artist's work is an essential part of an integrated whole. Collaboration thus occurs in conception, planning, and execution of a complete work. In this process, artists functioning singly and in groups regularly draw upon knowledge and expertise from the sciences, humanities, and social sciences.

Collaboration is also increasing across the arts and other disciplines in teaching, research, and scholarship. Multi- and interdisciplinary work is a common goal. These collaborations regularly occur as arts-related issues are pursued within and among the various perspectives outlined previously.

Since collaboration requires synthesis, new approaches, new processes, and new ways of thinking are regularly discovered. Collaboration thus energizes artistic and intellectual development.

Professional and Public Review

It is essential for faculty to place their work before professional communities and the public; however, those who make art may "publish" in formats quite different from those who study art and its impact. Although each institution will create its own definitions for evaluative and other purposes, performance, presentation, or installation of works of art serve the same function for those who work *in* art as publication in article or book form serves for those who do work *about* art.

Priorities

Each institution and academic unit concerned with the arts establishes priorities on many levels. Fundamental priorities are developed about the extent to which the arts will be present and what emphases will be given to specific arts. Within disciplines, some institutions focus on preparing artists; others, on preparing scholars; still others, on preparing teachers. Some do all three and more.

Priorities are also established regarding the scope of disciplinary coverage. These decisions regularly control which elements of a discipline and its subdisciplines are means and which are ends in specific curricula. For example, the study of drawing can have a different relationship to the work of the prospective painter than to the work of the prospective designer or landscape architect.

Relationships between studies and activities associated with making, studying, and teaching art are also profoundly affected by decisions about scope and focus. Since priorities are directly related to mission, goals, and objectives, they constitute one framework for decisions concerning the work of the faculty.

Faculty Responsibilities

Within the context provided by mission, goals, objectives, and priorities, faculties undertake specific responsibilities. These involve particular focuses and interrelationships regarding:

▶   Teaching that enables students to gain skills in and understanding of the media, processes, techniques, histories, and interdisciplinary relationships that comprise work in the arts disciplines, and to develop creative insight and critical judgment in aesthetic decision-making.

▶ Creative work and research associated with making new things, discovering how things work, understanding what happened, and revealing what things mean.

▶ Service that brings expertise to the work of the institution, the profession, and the larger community.

In teaching, creative work, research, and service, art may be approached from single or multiple perspectives: process, product, educative force, communication, psychological phenomenon, physiological phenomenon, therapeutics, social expression, heritage, subject matter for other disciplines, and so forth.

Some faculty members focus their efforts on an exclusive area of specialization; however, many faculty address more than one area. Whatever the degree of specialization or the content involved, all faculty work, including preparations for teaching and service, can utilize the processes of creation, discovery, analysis, integration, synthesis, application, and evaluation common to all intellectually based activity.

Arts faculty are regularly involved with one-on-one instruction characterized by constant evaluation as a work or presentation is made. Fulfilling this responsibility requires the ability to motivate, challenge, support, and direct individual students.

In practice, each faculty member has a specific profile of responsibilities showing relationships among such factors as competence, teaching assignments, area of creative or scholarly expertise, and philosophy about the role and purpose of the discipline. This profile may change constantly due to such influences as professional growth and institutional development. Interactions among these factors create the individual faculty member's approach to teaching, creative work and research, and service. Individual approaches are also deeply influenced by the nature of the field, the nature of traditions surrounding the field, and the nature of real or perceived expectations within the institution.

The above considerations demonstrate the infinite possibilities for developing sets of specific faculty responsibilities and expectations. For example, preparation of professionals in the arts disciplines requires teaching and learning about making new things, discovering how things work, understanding what happened, and revealing what things mean. Each faculty member will contribute by fulfilling a different set of responsibilities with respect to these activities. Thus, policies regarding faculties in the arts disciplines cannot be one-dimensional unless goals and objectives are centered around only one highly specialized activity. Determinations and evaluations of faculty responsibilities must be crafted according to the number of dimensions within the discipline covered by goals and objectives. These determinations and evaluations include attention to the elements, responsibilities, and perspectives previously covered.

III. Evaluation Issues

Defining Responsibilities

Effective and fair evaluation is based on clear and accurate statements regarding responsibilities and expectations. Such statements are critical because evaluations made by colleagues in the discipline, by students, by the institution, and by the individual faculty member can be quite different. For example, magnificent teaching as recognized by students may not carry significant weight with colleagues or with the institution. It is also important to be clear about the weight given various duties and perspectives — art as process, product, educative force, and so forth. This is particularly important when faculty members undertake vital responsibilities in the less glamorous or visible aspects of the profession. If a particular faculty responsibility is essential to the viability of the discipline, to development of students' fundamental competencies, and to the credibility of an institution's curriculum, then fulfillment of that responsibility should be judged on the basis of its importance rather than its stereotyped image.

Dealing With Complexity

If creation of new work and discovery of new knowledge are critical to the mission of an institution, evaluation mechanisms must have the capability to deal with various complex juxtapositions of perspective, technical competence, and inspiration that appear as these goals are pursued in the arts disciplines. The evaluation process must be able to deal with the objective and subjective natures of the arts. It must also account for the various imperatives involved in making art, studying art, and studying the impact of art, and for the interrelationship of all three. It must be able to deal with this interrelationship without pretending that one component is a substitute for another. It must be able to work with the arts both on their own terms and in terms appropriate to the humanities, the sciences, and the social sciences.

Determining Merit

Evaluation processes yield judgments about merit. Merit can be self-defined or defined by others. Whatever criteria are used, it is essential to consider merit in terms of goals, objectives, priorities, and mission. All such considerations may proceed from the perspective of the institution and the arts unit, or they may proceed from the perspectives of the discipline, of students, or of the individual faculty member. In any case, the particular arrangement of elements and perspectives used to determine merit must be considered and articulated as clearly as possible, especially at the time of faculty appointment.

Rewarding Teaching

Values concerning the role and purpose of teaching in cultural development are critical in every field. The connection between teaching and cultural development has particular impact on the arts because work in the arts disciplines profoundly influences the cultural context that envelops and affects decisions and events. Since all work in the arts disciplines has multiple connections with education and cultural formation, teaching assumes particular importance. Evaluation policies and procedures should account for this fact, so central to the nature and function of the arts within academe and in society as a whole.

Providing Opportunities

Institutions provide significant support to the work of arts faculty. However, the nature, scope, and availability of creative and research opportunities must be factors in considering productivity within a discipline. For example, the disparity between external research funding available to the arts and humanities in comparison to the sciences is beyond the control of institutions, academic units, or faculty members. Disparities can also occur with respect to release time and to opportunities for peer review when work cannot be distributed and studied in print form.

Focusing on Work

Modern public relations techniques make it possible to substitute fame for achievement, to confuse source or place with quality, and to confuse technical production features with content. Association with images of achievement is not achievement in and of itself. Images of quality are not a substitute for quality. Important work in the arts is not always immediately appreciated. Concepts such as "national recognition" need to be defined and used with care, since meaning may vary among disciplines, subdisciplines, institutions, and academic units.

Considering Innovation

Evaluative dilemmas can arise when disproportionate emphasis is placed on innovation, especially on innovation as the only goal. These dilemmas are particularly evident in the arts, where the most sophisticated evaluations cannot be based on empirical criteria, and where there is often no basis for comparison. It can be difficult to distinguish between genuine and apparent innovation, between new knowledge and new jargon, between fad initiation and aesthetic advancement. Multiple expert perspectives are useful in making these distinctions, but evaluation systems should avoid superficial use of the term "innovation." They should also avoid attempts to use a common definition of innovation across the arts, sciences, humanities, and social sciences.

Working With Equivalencies

The complexity of issues involved in the work of faculty members makes it impossible to establish exact equivalencies across academic disciplines. Policies designed to address equivalency should be consistent with the natures of the disciplines involved *and* with the mission, goals, and objectives of the institution. Methods can be devised to promote fairness. But no method in and of itself can produce empirical equivalency and ensure both fairness and a quality result at the same time.

Equivalencies are particularly difficult to formulate between work *in* and work *about* the arts disciplines. The challenge is to produce a reasonable policy based on specific goals and objectives while avoiding using one set of criteria as a template for the other.

Monitoring Technique

Overemphasis on specific assessment techniques can produce conditions where both work and evaluation are considered only in terms of what favored technologies and techniques can do. In these conditions, work and evaluation having no mathematical base, or foreign to the techniques of a particular assessment, can be discounted; goals and objectives fundamental to the work of a discipline or an academic unit can go unfulfilled, or be lost altogether. Effective evaluation of arts faculties depends on balancing technological means and technological thinking with other intellectual approaches.

Honoring Expertise

Each decision-maker in higher education has values concerning the work of faculty derived from his or her own discipline and from perspectives gained by observing work in other disciplines. Although decision-makers are required to make judgments that affect areas outside their disciplinary expertise, policies, evaluation methodologies, and protocols go only so far. There can be no substitute for the expertise of individuals within a discipline. Local efforts to define and reward the work of the faculty should place fundamental reliance on discipline-based expertise.

IV. ADVICE TO USERS

The information and ideas contained in this document will be applied differently in each institution and arts unit. Mission, goals, objectives, priorities, and values influence these applications. The following points may be useful in local policy-making.

▶ This text demonstrates the large number of possibilities for the work of faculty members singly or as a group. It describes the intermingling of functions, duties, and aspirations. It demonstrates that many approaches and responsibilities are usually present in a single individual. In this context, compartmentalizing seems counterproductive. Scholarship and artistry are not mutually exclusive.

▶ No faculty member should be expected to demonstrate equal accomplishment in all areas identified in this document.

▶ Intellectual work carried out by individuals working as artists, scholars, researchers, and teachers covers a broad range of activities, approaches, and perspectives. Although the existence of this breadth is undeniable, institutions determine through their policies and operations the specific type or types of intellectual work they wish to promote and support. Such determinations should be consistent with goals, objectives, mission, and resources.

▶ Definitions and priorities regarding the work of arts faculty are a unique, local matter. Emphasis should be on deriving policies from purposes and goals rather than copying perceived or actual practices at other institutions.

▶ Decisions should be made and published about the extent to which definitions of terms will be broad or narrow, and these decisions should inform discussion and policy development.

▶ Each institution is responsible for defining positions and responsibilities for teaching, creative work and research, and service. In the arts disciplines it is often difficult to categorize activities in these areas. For example, to what extent is a faculty performance on campus teaching, creative work, or service? Does the answer change if the performance is given elsewhere? These questions are particularly critical with respect to artistic directors, conductors, coaches, choreographers, and theatrical designers, and the answers for each campus should be clearly developed and specified.

▶ Documentation policies are critical aspects of fair and effective evaluation. They must fit logically into the larger policy equation that creates a viable relationship among aspirations, programs, and resources. Documentation policies should account for different definitions and formats for public presentation of work, and should be consistent with the basic nature of the work being evaluated. Clear definition and publication of these policies are essential.

▶ Policy changes associated with use of this report should enrich and enhance possibilities for mixtures of approaches and responsibilities. Initial goals should be to evaluate priorities, increase options, and to clarify responsibilities of the faculty.

▶ Care is needed to ensure that complex ideas and objectives are not devalued through superficial, casual, or repetitive use of terms such as "integration," "synthesis," and "creativity."

▶ Time is limited; work is seemingly unlimited. Work involving creation, discovery, analysis, interpretation, integration, synthesis, application, and evaluation is time-intensive. Caution must be exercised lest expectations for faculty in the arts become too great for dedicated individuals to fulfill. Attention is especially needed where faculty must work collaboratively with other faculty and students. Such activities, when a part of or combined with teaching, can leave little time for individual research and creative work. The time requirements of all positions, assignments, and expectations must be carefully considered as goals, objectives, action plans, and policies are developed.

▶ Most teaching associated with art involves continuous supervision and assessment of work in progress. It often demands time-consuming involvement with the presentation of student work. Policies regarding arts faculties should accept and respond to these realities.

▶ In setting goals, objectives, and policies, faculty and administrators should ensure that individuals are evaluated on the basis of their budgeted position and their described duties. Positions and duties should have clear relationships to mission, goals, and objectives regarding teaching, creative work and research, and service: relationships among all these should produce an equation that balances on its own terms and also in terms of time available. As institutions review their purposes and operations against goals and objectives for teaching, creative work and research, and service, first considerations should be given to the viability of current priorities and the prospect of additional options for creative and effective evaluation.

V. THE WORK OF ARTS FACULTIES

The following outline** presents a composite list of responsibilities undertaken by various faculty in each of the arts disciplines. This common outline is used as the basis for each of the discipline-specific outlines that follow. Users should note the following:

▶ **The excitement, power, and achievement of great teaching, creative work-research, and service come from individual expertise, inspiration, and involvement, and from institutional support. This document can only note these possibilities; realizing them is an individual and local matter.**

▶ **Users may wish to rearrange the outline or double list categories such as administration, grant writing, adjudication, consulting, etc., to better fit their mission, goals, and objectives.**

▶ **This document assumes a commitment to introduce students to works and techniques from various world cultures and historical periods.**

Teaching

The combination of content, intellectual processes, approaches, and preparations that produce instruction and associated services for students at the institution. Each faculty member undertakes a judicious selection of the following:

Delivering Group or Individual Instruction That Enables Students to

▶ Make Art
  — develop knowledge and skills in the practice of an arts discipline
  — integrate and synthesize knowledge and skills in the creation or performance of a work of art

▶ Study, Understand, and Evaluate Art, Its Influences, and Its Relationships
  — analyze how works of art function as artistic and aesthetic entities

---

** PLEASE NOTE: Every item in this outline involves to some degree any or all of the following: (1) Intellectual processes: creation, discovery, analysis, interpretation, integration, synthesis, application, evaluation, etc. (2) Approaches to [art, architecture, art/design, dance, film/video, landscape architecture, music, theatre] as: process, product, educative force, communication, psychological phenomenon, physiological phenomenon, therapeutics, social expression, heritage, subject matter for other disciplines, etc. (3) Connections and interrelationships among the various categories and items in the outline. Choices in these matters are at times institutional, at times individual, and at times both.

- — understand the history of an arts discipline, including the impact of specific works on the discipline itself
- — analyze the past and present relationships of art with events, ideas, people, and situations as studied through the methodologies and theories of the humanities, social sciences, and natural sciences
▶ Teach Art
- — integrate and synthesize knowledge, skills, and techniques in the development and delivery of instruction
▶ Apply Art and Facilitate Arts Activities
- — practice in fields involving connections between the arts and such areas as administration, commerce, public relations, therapies, and technologies

Preparing for Group or Individual Instruction
▶ Maintaining artistic and intellectual currency in the discipline
▶ Creating, discovering, integrating, synthesizing, and applying ideas, subject matter, and technique for specific instructional applications
▶ Designing, administering, coordinating, and supervising student projects, productions, and research

Evaluating
▶ Measuring the development of student competence
▶ Assessing personal effectiveness
▶ Appraising course and student project results in light of goals and objectives

Advising
▶ Advising students regarding curricula and projects
▶ Providing guidance and direction in the field
▶ Mentoring students toward achievement of diverse professional goals

Creative Work and Research

The combination of individual work in the discipline and its presentation in exhibitions, performances, productions, and publications in various formats. Each faculty member undertakes a judicious single or multiple selection among the following:

Making Art
▶ Creating a work of art
▶ Performing a work of art
▶ Developing new technologies, techniques, and approaches that advance creative capabilities

Studying Art and Its Influences

▶ Analyzing how works of art function internally

▶ Investigating and understanding the history and impact of an arts discipline

▶ Researching and understanding the physiological and psychological impacts of art

▶ Exploring the sociological impact of art

▶ Creating and assessing ideas and values about art — aesthetics, criticism, and philosophy

▶ Considering the multiple influences on art from various sources

▶ Integrating and synthesizing some or all of the above

Advancing the Pedagogy of Art

▶ Developing instructional materials and curricula that have broad impact on the field

▶ Determining causes and effects in educational settings

▶ Integrating and applying theoretical and practical knowledge in policy settings

▶ Exploring philosophical, sociological, and historical connections between the arts and education

Applying Art and Facilitating Arts Activities

▶ Curating, exhibiting, programming, publishing, and recording works of art

▶ Exploring and developing connections between art and such areas as administration, commerce, public relations, and technologies

▶ Developing and practicing arts therapies

▶ Exhibiting, programming, and publishing explanations, studies, and critiques; research and scholarly findings; translations and compilations

Service

The utilization of disciplinary and other expertise to support and advance the institution, the discipline, and the community. Each faculty member undertakes a judicious single or multiple selection among the following:

Assisting the Institution

▶ Organizing, coordinating, administering, or maintaining curricular programs, academic departments, campus organizations, technical facilities, or institutional events

▶ Serving on committees

▶ Identifying and writing grant proposals; fund raising

▶ Recruiting students and faculty

▶ Appraising institutional and departmental results in light of goals and objectives

▶ Providing expertise that assists the work of other institutional units, including libraries, academic and administrative departments, development offices, and support agencies

Advancing the Profession Beyond the Institution

▶ Organizing, coordinating, or administering exhibitions, performances, projects, organizations, or events
▶ Professional writing
▶ Editing
▶ Serving on committees, task forces, review and advisory boards, councils
▶ Adjudicating and reviewing
▶ Consulting

Contributing to the Community

▶ Participating in working groups, boards, arts councils, and community events
▶ Consulting, clinical work, and practice in the community
▶ Contributing to public education through teaching, performances, and presentations

THE WORK OF THE ARCHITECTURE FACULTY

The following outline** [see previous note] presents a composite list of responsibilities undertaken by architecture faculty. Users should note the following:

▶ The excitement, power, and achievement of great teaching, creative work-research, and service come from individual expertise, inspiration, and involvement, and from institutional support. This document can only note these possibilities; realizing them is an individual and local matter.

▶ Users may wish to rearrange the outline or double list categories such as administration, grant writing, adjudication, consulting, etc., to better fit their mission, goals, and objectives.

▶ This document assumes a commitment to introduce students to works and techniques from various world cultures and historical periods.

Users of the outline may obtain a more comprehensive picture by considering these activities in relation to various approaches and perspectives for content outlined in Section II.

Italics are used to indicate a few primary examples in each category.

Teaching

The combination of content, intellectual processes, approaches, and preparations that produce instruction and associated services for students at the institution. Each faculty member undertakes a judicious selection of the following:

Delivering Group or Individual Instruction That Enables Students to

▶ Create Architectural Designs and Works

— develop knowledge, problem-solving abilities, and skills in architecture and the practice of architectural design and works. This may include social, environmental, technical, theoretical, and aesthetic aspects of architectural design

— integrate and synthesize knowledge and skills in the creation of architectural designs and works

sketches, drawings, models, specifications; written, verbal, and visual presentations

▶ Study, Understand, and Evaluate Architecture

— analyze how architecture functions as aesthetic and practical entities

architectural theory; social, environmental, technical, aesthetic aspects, and cultural contexts

— understand the histories and theories of architecture

historical description and analysis; bibliography and impact of specific works on the discipline

— understand architecture as studied through other methodologies

sociology of architecture; psychology of architecture; anthropology, philosophy, and the natural and physical sciences

▶ Teach Architecture

— integrate and synthesize knowledge, skills, and techniques in the development and delivery of instruction

▶ Practice Architecture

— make connections among architecture, business practice and management, and law and regulations

These aspects of teaching are delivered through individual and group instruction, preparation for and presentation of exhibitions and student projects, seminars, and in informal settings.

Preparing for Group or Individual Instruction

▶ Maintaining artistic and intellectual currency in the discipline *creative work and research; independent, private, or group study; professional exchange*

▶ Creating, discovering, integrating, synthesizing, and applying ideas, subject matter, and technique for specific instructional applications
course and project development

▶ Designing, administering, coordinating, and supervising student projects
design projects; theses; dissertations

Evaluating

▶ Measuring the development of student competence
designs; projects; examinations

▶ Assessing personal effectiveness
studio, classroom, and informal teaching

▶ Appraising course and student project results in light of goals and objectives
course and curricula review

Advising

▶ Advising students regarding curricula and projects

▶ Providing guidance and direction in the field

▶ Mentoring students toward achievement of diverse professional goals

Creative Work and Research

The combination of individual work in architecture and its presentation in exhibitions, performances, productions, and publications in various formats. Each faculty member undertakes a judicious single or multiple selection among the following:

Creating Architectural Designs

research and synthesis that lead to original architectural and related designs by means of commissions, contracts, competitions, and proposals

Studying Architecture and Studying Its Influences

▶ Analyzing how works of architecture function
theory; technology

▶ Investigating the history and impact of architecture
studies and analyses from historical, geographical, cultural, religious, and other perspectives; history of architectural ideas; bibliography

▶ Researching the physiological and psychological impact of architecture
behavioral studies

▶ Exploring the sociological impact of architecture

architecture and society; ethnographic and demographic studies
▶ Creating and assessing ideas and values about architecture
aesthetics, criticism, and philosophy of architecture
▶ Considering the multiple influences on architecture from various sources
conditions, events, ideas, and technologies
▶ Integrating and synthesizing some or all of the above

Advancing the Pedagogy of Architecture
▶ Developing instructional materials and curricula that have broad impact on the field
▶ Determining causes and effects in educational settings
▶ Integrating and applying theoretical and practical knowledge in educational policy settings
▶ Exploring philosophical, sociological, and historical connections between architecture and education

Applying Architecture and Facilitating Architectural Activities
▶ Exhibiting and publishing architectural designs, plans, drawings, models, and photographs
▶ Exhibiting, programming, and publishing explanations, studies, and critiques; research and scholarly findings; translations and compilations
books and chapters in books; articles, monographs; delivering or publishing conference papers, panel discussions, proceedings; lectures; reviews of books, exhibitions, or new works of architecture; appointments as artist-in-residence; workshops; master classes; interviews; seminars; computer applications
▶ Exploring and developing connections between the discipline and practice of architecture
business practice and management; law and regulations

Service

The utilization of disciplinary and other expertise to support and advance the institution, architecture, and the community. Each faculty member undertakes a judicious single or multiple selection among the following:

Assisting the Institution
▶ Organizing, coordinating, administering, or maintaining curricular programs, academic departments, campus organizations, technical facilities, or institutional events
▶ Serving on committees

▶ Identifying and writing grant proposals; fund raising

▶ Recruiting students and faculty

▶ Appraising institutional and departmental results in light of goals and objectives

▶ Providing expertise that assists the work of other institutional units, including libraries, academic and administrative departments, development offices, and support agencies

Advancing the Profession Beyond the Institution

▶ Organizing, coordinating, or administering exhibitions, projects, organizations, or events

▶ Professional writing

▶ Editing

▶ Serving on committees, task forces, review and advisory boards, councils

▶ Adjudicating and reviewing

▶ Consulting

Contributing to the Community

▶ Participating in working groups, boards, professional organizations, arts councils, and community events

▶ Consulting and practice in the community

▶ Contributing to public education through teaching and presentations

THE WORK OF THE ART AND DESIGN FACULTY

The following outline** [see previous note] presents a composite list of responsibilities undertaken by art and design faculty. Users should note the following:

▶ The excitement, power, and achievement of great teaching, creative work-research, and service come from individual expertise, inspiration, and involvement, and from institutional support. This document can only note these possibilities; realizing them is an individual and local matter.

▶ Users may wish to rearrange the outline or double list categories such as administration, grant writing, adjudication, consulting, etc., to better fit their mission, goals, and objectives.

▶ This document assumes a commitment to introduce students to works and techniques from various world cultures and historical periods.

  Users of the outline may obtain a more comprehensive picture by considering these activities in relation to various approaches and perspectives for content

outlined in Section II.
Italics **are used to indicate a few primary examples in each category.**

Teaching

The combination of content, intellectual processes, approaches, and preparations that produce instruction and associated services for students at the institution. Each faculty member undertakes a judicious selection of the following:

Delivering Group or Individual Instruction That Enables Students to

▶ Make Art and Design
   — develop knowledge and skills in the practice of art, design, and related disciplines
      develop an understanding of art and design principles, concepts, materials and processes; techniques and insights for solving aesthetic and design problems; use of art and design technologies, including computers
   — integrate and synthesize knowledge, skills, and understanding in the creation of a work of art or design
      creating works of art and design in such areas as advertising design; ceramics; commercial design; drawing; fashion design; film/video; glass; graphic design; illustration; industrial design; interior design; jewelry/metals; painting; photography; printmaking; sculpture; textile/surface design; theatre design; weaving/fibers; woodworking; performance art

▶ Study, Understand, and Evaluate Art and Design Disciplines, Their Influences, and Their Relationships
   — analyze how art and design works function as artistic and aesthetic entities
      visual theory: perspective, form, color, composition, shape and texture, value, scale, motion, the impact of technology
   — understand the history of art and design including the impact of specific works on the disciplines themselves
      historical description and analysis; bibliography; style; current contexts; evolution of techniques
   — analyze past and present relationships of art and design with events, ideas, people, and situations as studied through various methodologies and theories
      aesthetics; sociology of art; psychology of art; art therapy; art-design criticism and theory; relationships to general history

▶ Teach Art and Design
   — integrate and synthesize knowledge, skills, and techniques in the understanding,

development, and delivery of instruction

> *teaching skills; educational methodologies; evaluation; course and curriculum development; instructional innovation; research; development and preparation of instructional materials*

▶ Apply Art and Design and Facilitate Art and Design Activities

— practice in fields involving connections between art and design and such areas as administration, commerce, public relations, and technologies

> *museum and gallery management; commercial art; art and design industries; artist management; copyright and patent issues; art therapy; art and design technologies*

These aspects of teaching are delivered through individual and group instruction, preparation for and presentation of exhibitions and installations, master classes/guest artists, seminars, and in informal settings.

Preparing for Group or Individual Instruction

▶ Maintaining artistic and intellectual standards in the discipline

> *creative work and research; independent, individual, or group study; professional exchange*

▶ Creating, discovering, understanding, integrating, synthesizing, and applying ideas, subject matter, and technique for specific instructional applications

> *course and project development*

▶ Designing, administering, coordinating, and supervising student projects

> *research; portfolio development projects; exhibitions; theses; dissertations*

Evaluating

▶ Assessing the development of student learning

> *group or individual critiques; portfolio reviews; written projects; examinations*

▶ Assessing personal effectiveness

> *studio, classroom, individual, and independent teaching*

▶ Appraising course and student project results in light of goals and objectives

> *course and curricula review*

Advising

▶ Advising students regarding curricula and projects

▶ Providing guidance and direction in art and design relative to career goals and professional development

▶ Mentoring students toward achievement of diverse professional goals

Creative Work and Research

The combination of individual work in the visual arts and its presentation in exhibitions, performances, productions, and publications in various formats. Each faculty member undertakes a judicious single or multiple selection among the following:

Creating Art and Design

▶ Creating works of art and design

study, research, understanding, and synthesis that result in original works of art and design

▶ Developing new technologies, techniques, and approaches that advance creative capabilities in art and design

Studying Art and Design

▶ Analyzing art work

visual theory and other critical dimensions

▶ Investigating the history and impact of art and design

studies and analyses from historical, geographical, cultural, ethnic, religious, and other perspectives; history of art and design ideas; bibliography

▶ Researching the psychological impact of art and design

visual perception; behavioral applications

▶ Exploring the sociological impact of art and design

art-design and the human condition; art-design and society; ethnographic and demographic studies

▶ Creating and assessing ideas and values about art and design

aesthetics; criticism; philosophy

▶ Considering the multiple influences on art and design from various sources

conditions, events, ideas, and technologies

▶ Integrating and synthesizing some or all of the above

Advancing the Pedagogy of Art and Design

▶ Developing instructional materials and curricula that have broad impact on the field
▶ Determining causes and effects in educational settings
▶ Integrating and applying theoretical and practical knowledge in educational policy settings
▶ Exploring philosophical, sociological, and historical connections between art and design and education

Applying Art and Design and Facilitating Art and Design Activities

▶ Curating, exhibiting, and publishing works of art and design *curating or serving as artistic director of exhibitions; festivals; summer programs; workshops; master classes; seminars*

▶ Exploring and developing connections between art and design and such areas as administration, commerce, public relations, and technologies

museum and gallery management; commercial art; art and design industries; artist management; copyright issues; art and design technologies

▶ Exhibiting, programming, and publishing explanations, studies, and critiques; research and scholarly findings; translations and compilations

books and chapters in books; articles, monographs; delivering or publishing conference papers, panel discussions, proceedings; lectures; reviews of books, exhibitions, installations, or new works of art; appointments as artist-in-residence; workshops; master classes; interviews; seminars; computer applications

▶ Developing and practicing art therapy

Service

The utilization of disciplinary and other expertise to support and advance the institution, the visual arts, and the community. Each faculty member undertakes a judicious single or multiple selection among the following:

Assisting the Institution

▶ Organizing, coordinating, administering, or maintaining curricular programs, academic departments and other units, technical facilities, campus organizations, or institutional events

▶ Serving on committees

▶ Identifying and writing grant proposals; fund raising

▶ Recruiting students and faculty

▶ Appraising institutional and departmental results in light of goals and objectives

▶ Providing expertise that assists the work of other institutional units, including libraries, academic and administrative departments, development offices, and support agencies

Advancing the Profession Beyond the Institution

▶ Organizing, coordinating, or administering exhibitions, performances, projects, organizations, or events

▶ Professional writing

▶ Editing

▶ Serving on committees, task forces, review and advisory boards, and councils

▶ Adjudicating and reviewing

▶ Consulting

Contributing to the Community

▶ Participating in working groups, boards, arts councils, and community events
▶ Consulting, clinical work, and practice in the community
▶ Contributing to public education through teaching and exhibitions

THE WORK OF THE DANCE FACULTY

The following outline** [see previous note] presents a composite list of responsibilities undertaken by dance faculty. Users should note the following:

▶ **The excitement, power, and achievement of great teaching, creative work-research, and service come from individual expertise, inspiration, and involvement, and from institutional support. This document can only note these possibilities; realizing them is an individual and local matter.**
▶ **Users may wish to rearrange the outline or double list categories such as administration, grant writing, adjudication, consulting, etc., to better fit their mission, goals, and objectives.**
▶ **This document assumes a commitment to introduce students to works and techniques from various world cultures and historical periods.**

Users of the outline may obtain a more comprehensive picture by considering these activities in relation to various approaches and perspectives for content outlined in Section II.

***Italics* are used to indicate a few primary examples in each category.**

Teaching

The combination of content, intellectual processes, approaches, and preparations that produce instruction and associated services for students at the institution. Each faculty member undertakes a judicious selection of the following:

Delivering Group or Individual Instruction That Enables Students to

▶ Dance
— develop knowledge and skills in the practice of dance and dance-related disciplines
choreography; dance sciences and somatics; dance techniques (ballet, ethnic, folk, jazz, modern, etc.); improvisation; movement analysis; music; notation and other analytical and reconstructive skills; production design
— integrate and synthesize knowledge and skills in the creation, reconstruction, and/

or performance of a work of dance

> *choreographing original work; reconstructing repertory; directing; preparing and presenting dance in concert and other settings*

▶ Study, Understand, and Evaluate Dance, Its Influences, and Its Relationships

— analyze works of dance as artistic and aesthetic entities

> *dance theory, philosophy, and criticism; anatomy and kinesiology; dance notation*

— understand genres of dance, including cultural context and the impact of specific works on the discipline itself

> *style; repertory; historical description and analysis; dance ethnology; bibliography; evolution of technique or form*

— analyze past and present relationships of dance with events, ideas, people, and situations

> *history of dance; philosophy of dance; sociology of dance; psychology of dance; and related methodologies and theories of other fields such as humanities, social sciences, and natural sciences; relationships to general history and culture*

▶ Teach Dance

— integrate and synthesize knowledge, skills, and techniques in the development and delivery of instruction

> *teaching skills; educational methodologies; evaluation; course and curriculum development; instructional innovation; research; development and preparation of instructional materials*

▶ Apply Dance and Facilitate Dance Activities

— practice in fields involving connections between dance and such areas as administration, commerce, public relations, therapies, and technologies

> *administration of presenting organizations and venues; artist management; dance therapy; media arts*

These aspects of teaching are delivered through individual and group instruction, preparation for and presentation of dance concerts and productions, master classes, seminars, and in informal settings.

Preparing for Group or Individual Instruction

▶ Maintaining artistic and intellectual activity and standing in the discipline

> *creative work and research; independent, private, or group study; professional exchange and presentation*

▶ Creating, discovering, integrating, synthesizing, and applying ideas, subject matter,

and technique for specific instructional applications
> *course and project development; rehearsal preparation*

▶ Directing, designing, administering, coordinating, and supervising student projects and productions
> *auditions; choreographing; designing; dissertations; rehearsing; research; technical directing; theses; concert advising*

Evaluating

▶ Measuring the development of student competence
> *entrance auditions; periodic adjudication; dance concerts; juries; written and video projects; examinations*

▶ Assessing personal effectiveness
> *studio, classroom, and informal teaching*

▶ Appraising course and student project results in light of goals and objectives
> *course and curricula review*

Advising

▶ Advising students regarding curricula and projects
▶ Providing guidance and direction in the field
▶ Mentoring students toward achievement of diverse professional goals
▶ Referring students to appropriate specialists in areas such as nutrition, care and prevention of injuries, body conditioning, and related health matters

Creative Work and Research

The combination of individual work in dance and its presentation in performances, productions, publications, and exhibitions in various formats. Each faculty member undertakes a judicious single or multiple selection among the following:

Creating Dance

▶ Performing
> *practice, study, and rehearsal that lead to live, film, or video performance of solo or ensemble dances*

▶ Choreographing and/or reconstructing a work of dance
> *study, research, and synthesis that lead to original or reconstructed works of dance*

▶ Directing
> *study of repertory; directorial techniques; coaching*

▶ Developing new technologies, techniques, and approaches that advance creative capabilities in dance

Studying Dance and Its Influences

▶ Analyzing works of dance as artistic and aesthetic entities
  dance aesthetics; critical theory; movement analysis

▶ Researching the history and impact of dance
  repertory; studies and analyses from historical, geographical, cultural, anthropological, religious, and other perspectives; history of dance ideas; performance practices; bibliography

▶ Researching the physiological and psychological impact of dance
  anatomy and kinesiology; therapeutic applications; somatic studies

▶ Researching the sociological impact of dance
  dance and the human condition; dance and society; ethnographic and demographic studies; marketing

▶ Creating and assessing ideas and values about dance
  aesthetics, criticism, and philosophy of dance

▶ Considering the multiple influences on dance from various sources
  conditions, events, ideas, and technologies

▶ Integrating and synthesizing some or all of the above

Advancing the Pedagogy of Dance

▶ Developing instructional materials and curricula that have broad impact on the field

▶ Determining causes and effects in educational settings

▶ Integrating and applying theoretical and practical knowledge in educational policy settings

▶ Exploring philosophical, sociological, and historical connections between dance and education

Applying Dance and Facilitating Dance Activities

▶ Exploring and developing connections between dance and such areas as administration, commerce, public relations, therapies, and technologies
  administration of presenting organizations and venues; touring; artist and repertory management; copyright; media arts

▶ Developing and practicing dance-movement therapy

▶ Programming and presenting dance
  producing and/or directing dance events such as festivals, summer programs, dance performance series, workshops, master classes, seminars

▶ Exhibiting, programming, and publishing explanations, studies, and critiques; research and scholarly findings; translations and compilations; notation of scores

> *books and chapters in books; articles; monographs; notated scores; delivering or publishing conference papers, panel discussions, proceedings; lectures; reviews of books, performances, productions, or new works of dance; appointments as artist-in-residence; performances as part of professional meetings; workshops; master classes; interviews; seminars; computer applications; program notes*

Service

The utilization of disciplinary and other expertise to support and advance the institution, dance, and the community. Each faculty member undertakes a judicious single or multiple selection among the following:

Assisting the Institution

▶ Organizing, coordinating, administering, or maintaining curricular programs, academic departments, campus organizations, technical facilities, or institutional events

▶ Serving on committees

▶ Identifying and writing grant proposals; fund raising

▶ Recruiting students and faculty

▶ Appraising institutional and departmental results in light of goals and objectives

▶ Mentoring junior faculty

▶ Providing expertise that assists the work of other institutional units, including libraries, academic and administrative departments, development offices, and support agencies

Advancing the Profession Beyond the Institution

▶ Organizing, coordinating, or administering exhibitions, performances, projects, organizations, or events

▶ Professional writing

▶ Editing

▶ Serving on committees, task forces, review and advisory boards, and councils

▶ Adjudicating and reviewing

▶ Consulting

Contributing to the Community

▶ Participating in working groups, boards, arts councils, and community events

▶ Consulting, clinical work, and practice in the community

▶ Contributing to public education through teaching, performances, and presentations

THE WORK OF THE FILM/VIDEO FACULTY

The following outline [see previous note] presents a composite list of responsibilities undertaken by film/video faculty. Users should note the following:**

▶ **The excitement, power, and achievement of great teaching, creative work-research, and service come from individual expertise, inspiration, and involvement, and from institutional support. This document can only note these possibilities; realizing them is an individual and local matter.**

▶ **Users may wish to rearrange the outline or double list categories such as administration, grant writing, adjudication, consulting, etc., to better fit their mission, goals, and objectives.**

▶ **This document assumes a commitment to introduce students to works and techniques from various world cultures and historical periods.**

Users of the outline may obtain a more comprehensive picture by considering these activities in relation to various approaches and perspectives for content outlined in Section II.

Italics **are used to indicate a few primary examples in each category.**

Teaching

The combination of content, intellectual processes, approaches, and preparations that produce instruction and associated services for students at the institution. Each faculty member undertakes a judicious selection of the following:

Delivering Group or Individual Instruction That Enables Students to

▶ Create Film/Video
— develop knowledge and skills in the practice of film/video
animation; cinematography; directing; editing; producing; sound; videography; screenwriting; production management
— integrate and synthesize knowledge, skills, ideas, and subject matter in the creation of film/video
documentary; fiction; experimental; animation; advertising; news; public relations; multimedia; computer applications (computer graphics, computer animation, interactive video)

▶ Study, Understand, and Evaluate Film/Video, Its Influences, and Its Relationships
— analyze how works of film/video function as practical and aesthetic entities
film/video theory; technical and aesthetic considerations

— understand the history of film/video, including the impact of specific works on the
discipline itself

*historical description and analysis; bibliography; development of techniques and
styles*

— analyze past and present relationships of film/video with events, ideas, people,
and situations as studied through the methodologies and theories of the humanities,
social sciences, and natural sciences

*philosophy of film/video; aesthetics; sociology of film/video; psychology of film/
video; film/video criticism; therapeutic applications; relationships to general
history*

▶ Teach Film/Video

— integrate and synthesize knowledge, skills, and techniques in the development and
delivery of instruction

*teaching skills; educational methodologies; evaluation; course and curriculum
development; instructional innovation; pedagogical issues; development and
preparation of instructional materials*

▶ Apply Film/Video and Facilitate Film/Video Activities

— practice in fields involving connections between film/video and such areas as
administration, public relations, therapies, and technologies

*business practices, commercial applications; marketing; broadcast law; artist
management; medical applications; educational applications*

These aspects of teaching are delivered through individual and group instruction,
preparation for and presentation of exhibitions and student projects, master classes,
seminars, and in informal settings.

Preparing for Group or Individual Instruction

▶ Maintaining artistic and intellectual currency in the discipline

creative work and research; independent or group study; professional exchange

▶ Creating, discovering, integrating, synthesizing, and applying ideas, subject matter,
and technique for specific instructional applications

course and project development

▶ Designing, administering, coordinating, and supervising student projects

productions; theses; dissertations

Evaluating

▶ Measuring the development of student competence

projects; examinations

THE ARTS

- ▶ Assessing personal effectiveness
  studio, classroom, and informal teaching
- ▶ Appraising course and student project results in light of goals and objectives
  course and curricula review

Advising
- ▶ Advising students regarding curricula and projects
- ▶ Providing guidance and direction in the field
- ▶ Mentoring students toward achievement of diverse professional goals

Creative Work and Research

The combination of individual work in film/video and its presentation in exhibitions, performances, productions, and publications in various formats. Each faculty member undertakes a judicious single or multiple selection among the following:

Making Film/Video
- ▶ Creating original works
  study, research, and synthesis that lead to original works of film/video involving skills and interdisciplinary relationships in animation; cinematography; computer graphics; directing; editing; funding; producing; screenwriting; sound recording; videography
- ▶ Collaborating within the discipline and with other disciplines in various aspects of a complete production
- ▶ Developing new technologies, techniques, and approaches that advance creative capabilities in film/video

Studying Film/Video and Its Influences
- ▶ Analyzing how works of film/video function
  film/video theory
- ▶ Investigating the history and impact of film/video
  studies and analyses from historical, geographical, cultural, religious, and other perspectives; history of film/video ideas; bibliography
- ▶ Researching the physiological and psychological impact of film/video
  audience research; behavioral studies; studies of propaganda
- ▶ Exploring the correlation between film/video and culture
  film/video and society; sociological, ethnographic, and demographic studies
- ▶ Creating and assessing ideas and values about film/video
  aesthetics; criticism; philosophy

- ▶ Considering the multiple influences on film/video from various sources
  conditions, events, ideas, and technologies
- ▶ Integrating and synthesizing some or all of the above

Advancing the Pedagogy of Film/Video
- ▶ Developing instructional materials and curricula that have broad impact on the field
- ▶ Determining causes and effects in educational settings
- ▶ Integrating and applying theoretical and practical knowledge in policy settings
- ▶ Exploring philosophical, sociological, and historical connections between film/video and education

Applying Film/Video and Facilitating Film/Video Activities
- ▶ Exhibiting and disseminating completed works
  festivals; conferences; competitions; galleries; museums; media arts centers; dissemination through distribution entities such as commercial, public, or cable television; distribution companies; university media libraries; arts organizations; professional associations; etc.
- ▶ Exhibiting, programming, and publishing explanations, studies, and critiques; research and scholarly findings; translations and compilations
  books and chapters in books; articles, monographs; delivering or publishing conference papers, panel discussions, proceedings; lectures; reviews of books or film/video; appointments as artist-in-residence; workshops; master classes; interviews; seminars; computer applications
- ▶ Curating, programming, and presenting film/video
  festivals; summer programs; film/video series; workshops; seminars
- ▶ Exploring and developing connections between film/video and such areas as administration, commerce, public relations, therapies, and technologies
  business practices, commercial applications, marketing; copyright; FCC regulations; artist management, medical applications; educational applications

Service
The utilization of disciplinary and other expertise to support and advance the institution, film/video, and the community. Each faculty member undertakes a judicious single or multiple selection among the following:

Assisting the Institution
- ▶ Organizing, coordinating, administering, or maintaining curricular programs, academic departments, campus organizations, technical facilities, or institutional events

- ▶ Serving on committees
- ▶ Identifying and writing grant proposals; fund raising
- ▶ Recruiting students and faculty
- ▶ Appraising institutional and departmental results in light of goals and objectives
- ▶ Providing expertise that assists the work of other institutional units, including libraries, academic and administrative departments, development offices, and support agencies

Advancing the Profession Beyond the Institution

- ▶ Organizing, coordinating, or administering exhibitions, performances, projects, organizations, or events
- ▶ Professional writing
- ▶ Editing
- ▶ Serving on committees, task forces, review and advisory boards, councils
- ▶ Adjudicating and reviewing
- ▶ Consulting

Contributing to the Community

- ▶ Participating in working groups, boards, arts councils, and community events
- ▶ Consulting and practice in the community
- ▶ Contributing to public education through teaching and presentations

THE WORK OF THE LANDSCAPE ARCHITECTURE FACULTY

The following outline** [see previous note] presents a composite list of responsibilities undertaken by landscape architecture faculty. Users should note the following:

- ▶ The excitement, power, and achievement of great teaching, creative work-research, and service come from individual expertise, inspiration, and involvement, and from institutional support. This document can only note these possibilities; realizing them is an individual and local matter.
- ▶ Users may wish to rearrange the outline or double list categories such as administration, grant writing, adjudication, consulting, etc., to better fit their mission, goals, and objectives.
- ▶ This document assumes a commitment to introduce students to works and techniques from various world cultures and historical periods.

Users of the outline may obtain a more comprehensive picture by considering these activities in relation to various approaches and perspectives for content outlined in Section II.

Italics **are used to indicate a few primary examples in each category.**

Teaching

The combination of content, intellectual processes, approaches, and preparations that produce instruction and associated services for students at the institution. Each faculty member undertakes a judicious selection of the following:

Delivering Group or Individual Instruction That Enables Students to

▶ Create Landscape Designs

— develop knowledge and skills in the practice of landscape architecture

natural and social sciences (horticulture, architecture, engineering, sociology, ecology, psychology, and anthropology); design; technology; aesthetics; written, graphic, and oral communication skills

— integrate and synthesize knowledge and skills in the creation of landscape designs at a range of scales

site planning; public park and open space design; urban design; master plans; landscape plans; community planning and design; commercial, industrial, and residential design

▶ Study, Understand, and Evaluate Landscape Architecture, Its Influences, and Its Relationships

— analyze how examples of landscape architecture operate as aesthetic and functional entities

landscape architectural theory; environmental, cultural, technical, and aesthetic aspects

— understand the history of landscape architecture, including the impact of specific designs on the discipline itself

historical description and analysis; development of techniques and styles; regional influences; bibliography

— analyze past and present relationships of landscape architecture with events, ideas, people, and situations as studied through the methodologies of the humanities, social sciences, and natural sciences

aesthetics; sociology of landscape architecture; psychology of landscape architecture; ecology of landscape architecture; relationships to general history

▶ Practice Landscape Architecture

— work in interdisciplinary terms with a range of professionals including engineers,

ecologists, archaeologists, architects, foresters, and regional planners
— practice landscape architecture in public and private settings

facilities and program management; contract and project management; data management; business practices and management; laws and regulations; technology; planning and policy development; communication of design solutions through drawings, models, computer simulations, and graphics

▶ Teach Landscape Architecture
— integrate and synthesize knowledge, skills, and techniques in the development and delivery of instruction

teaching skills; educational methodologies; evaluation; course and curriculum development; instructional innovation; pedagogical issues; development and preparation of instructional materials

These aspects of teaching are delivered through individual and group instruction, preparation for and presentation of exhibitions and student projects, seminars, and in informal settings.

Preparing for Studio or Class Instruction

▶ Maintaining artistic and intellectual currency in the discipline

creative work and research; independent, individual, or group study; professional exchange

▶ Creating, discovering, integrating, synthesizing, and applying ideas, subject matter, and technique for specific instructional applications

course and project development

▶ Designing, administering, coordinating, and supervising student projects

design projects; theses; dissertations

Evaluating

▶ Measuring the development of student competence

designs; projects; examinations; juries; design competitions

▶ Assessing personal effectiveness

studio, classroom, and informal teaching

▶ Appraising course and student project results in light of goals and objectives

course and curricula review

Advising

▶ Advising students regarding curricula and projects
▶ Providing guidance and direction in the field
▶ Mentoring students toward achievement of diverse professional goals

Creative Work and Research

The combination of individual work in landscape architecture and its presentation in exhibitions, performances, productions, and publications in various formats. Each faculty member undertakes a judicious single or multiple selection among the following:

Making Landscape Architecture

▶ Creating landscape designs

> *study, research, and synthesis that lead to original landscape designs (built works, proposed projects, design feasibility studies, competitions)*

▶ Performing landscape planning

> *master plans; management plans; ecosystem models; regional analyses; resource assessment; feasibility reports; visual management and sustainable landscape planning*

▶ Developing new technologies, techniques, and approaches that advance the capabilities of landscape architecture

Studying Landscape Architecture and Its Influences

▶ Evaluating landscape architectural designs

> *landscape architectural theory*

▶ Investigating the history and impact of landscape architecture

> *studies and analyses from historical, geographical, cultural, and other perspectives; history of ideas about landscape architecture; bibliography*

▶ Researching the social, economic, and environmental impact of landscape architecture

> *post-occupancy evaluation; visual analysis; landscape and human health; cross-cultural studies of landscape perception; user-needs analysis; cost-benefit analysis*

▶ Creating and assessing ideas and values about landscape architecture

> *aesthetics; criticism; philosophy; theory*

▶ Considering the multiple influences on landscape architecture from multiple perspectives

▶ Integrating and synthesizing all or some of the above

Applying and Presenting Landscape Architecture

▶ Exploring and developing connections between landscape architecture and such areas as administration, commerce, public relations, and technologies

> *business practices and management; law and regulations; technology*

▶ Exploring and developing methods of communicating design solutions

> *drawings and models; graphics; computer graphics and simulations*

▶ Exhibiting and publishing landscape architecture designs
▶ Exhibiting, programming, and publishing explanations, studies, and critiques; research and scholarly findings; translations and compilations

> *books and chapters in books; articles, monographs; delivering or publishing conference papers, panel discussions, proceedings; lectures; reviews of books or landscape architecture designs; appointments as artist-in-residence; workshops; master classes; interviews; seminars; computer applications*

Advancing the Pedagogy of Landscape Architecture

▶ Developing instructional materials and curricula that have broad impact on the field
▶ Determining causes and effects in educational settings
▶ Integrating and applying theoretical and practical knowledge in policy settings
▶ Exploring philosophical, sociological, and historical aspects of professional education

Service

The utilization of disciplinary and other expertise to support and advance the institution, landscape architecture, and the community. Each faculty member undertakes a judicious single or multiple selection among the following:

Assisting the Institution

▶ Organizing, coordinating, administering, or maintaining curricular programs, academic departments, campus organizations, technical facilities, or institutional events
▶ Serving on committees
▶ Identifying and writing grant proposals; fund raising
▶ Recruiting students and faculty
▶ Appraising institutional and departmental results in light of goals and objectives
▶ Providing expertise that assists the work of other institutional units, including libraries, academic and administrative departments, development offices, and support agencies

Advancing the Profession Beyond the Institution

▶ Organizing, coordinating, or administering exhibitions, competitions, projects, organizations, or events
▶ Professional writing
▶ Editing
▶ Serving on committees, task forces, review and advisory boards, councils
▶ Adjudicating and mediating

Contributing to the Community

▶ Participating in working groups, boards, arts councils, and community events

▶ Consulting and practice in the community

individual assistance; community assistance; classroom projects in service to the community

▶ Contributing to public education through teaching and exhibitions

THE WORK OF THE MUSIC FACULTY

The following outline** [see previous note] presents a composite list of responsibilities undertaken by music faculty. Users should note the following:

▶ **The excitement, power, and achievement of great teaching, creative work-research, and service come from individual expertise, inspiration, and involvement, and from institutional support. This document can only note these possibilities; realizing them is an individual and local matter.**

▶ **Users may wish to rearrange the outline or double list categories such as administration, grant writing, adjudication, consulting, etc., to better fit their mission, goals, and objectives.**

▶ **This document assumes a commitment to introduce students to works and techniques from various world cultures and historical periods.**

Users of the outline may obtain a more comprehensive picture by considering these activities in relation to various approaches and perspectives for content outlined in Section II.

***Italics* are used to indicate a few primary examples in each category.**

Teaching

The combination of content, intellectual processes, approaches, and preparations that produce instruction and associated services for students at the institution. Each faculty member undertakes a judicious selection of the following:

Delivering Group or Individual Instruction That Enables Students to

▶ **Make Music**

— develop knowledge and skills in the practice of music and music-related disciplines

musicianship; vocal, instrumental, conducting, compositional, and improvisational techniques; orchestration; interpretation; style; diction; movement; recording and computer technologies

— integrate and synthesize knowledge and skills in the creation or performance of musical works

composition; preparing and presenting recitals, concerts, religious services, and productions as arranger, composer, conductor, director, performer

▶ Study, Understand, and Evaluate Music, Its Influences, and Its Relationships

— examine how compositions function as artistic and aesthetic entities

music theory, including notations, harmony, counterpoint, and analysis

— understand the history of music, including the impact of specific works on the discipline itself

literature and repertory; historical description and analysis; bibliography; style; performance practices; evolution of compositional technique; cultural contexts and influences

— examine past and present relationships of music with events, ideas, people, and situations as studied through the methodologies and theories of the humanities, social sciences, and natural sciences

aesthetics; sociology of music; psychology of music; music therapy; acoustics; music criticism; relationships to general history

▶ Teach Music

— integrate and synthesize knowledge, skills, techniques, and technologies in the development and delivery of instruction

teaching skills; educational methodologies; evaluation; course and curriculum development; instructional innovation; research; development and preparation of instructional materials, including but not limited to use of electronic and computer capabilities

▶ Apply Music and Facilitate Music Activities

— work in fields involving connections between music and such areas as administration, arts management, public relations, therapies, and technologies

administration of presenting organizations and venues; commercial music; artist management; music therapy; recording arts; computer and electronic music

These aspects of teaching are delivered through individual and group instruction; preparation for and presentation of recitals, concerts, and staged productions; master classes; seminars; and in informal settings.

Preparing for Group or Individual Instruction

▶ Maintaining artistic and intellectual currency in the discipline

creative work and research; independent, private, or group study; professional exchange and development

▶ Creating, discovering, integrating, synthesizing, and applying ideas, subject matter, and technique for specific instructional applications

course and project development; rehearsal preparation

▶ Designing, administering, coordinating, and supervising student projects and productions

research; auditions; directing; rehearsing; choreographing; coaching; designing; technical directing; theses; dissertations

Evaluating

▶ Measuring the development of student competence

entrance auditions; recitals; competitions; juries; composition and performance portfolios; written projects; examinations

▶ Assessing personal effectiveness

studio, classroom, and informal teaching

▶ Appraising course and student project results in light of goals and objectives

course and curricula review

Advising

▶ Advising students regarding curricula and projects
▶ Providing guidance and direction in the field
▶ Mentoring students toward achievement of diverse professional goals

Creative Work and Research

The combination of individual work in music and its presentation in exhibitions, performances, productions, and publications in various formats. Each faculty member undertakes a judicious single or multiple selection among the following:

Making Music

▶ Performing

practice, study, research, and rehearsal leading to live or broadcast performances, film and videos, recordings, or competitions involving solo performances, ensemble performances, and conducting

▶ Creating a musical work

study, research, and synthesis leading to original works, transcriptions, and arrangements

▶ Improvising a musical work

performance combined with spontaneous creation

▶ Developing new technologies, techniques, and approaches that advance creative capabilities in music

Studying Music and Its Influences

▶ Analyzing compositions in terms of the compositional materials, structure, and expressive/communicative impact

▶ Investigating the history and impact of music

repertory; studies and analyses from historical, geographical, cultural, religious, and other perspectives; history of musical ideas, performance practices; bibliography

▶ Researching the physiological and psychological impact of music

musical perception and cognition; acoustics and psychoacoustics; therapeutic applications

▶ Exploring the sociological impact of music

music and the human condition; music and society; ethnographic and demographic studies; marketing; political influences

▶ Creating and assessing ideas and values about music

aesthetics, criticism, and philosophy of music

▶ Considering the multiple influences on music from various sources

conditions, events, ideas, and technologies

▶ Integrating and synthesizing some or all of the above

Advancing the Pedagogy of Music

▶ Developing, evaluating, and revising instructional materials and curricula having a broad impact on the field, including but not limited to computer and electronic applications

▶ Determining causes and effects in educational settings

▶ Integrating and applying theoretical and practical knowledge in educational policy settings

▶ Exploring philosophical, sociological, and historical connections between music and education

Applying Music and Facilitating Music Activities

▶ Exploring and developing connections between music and such areas as administration, arts management, public relations, therapies, and technologies

administration of presenting organizations and venues; music industries; artist and repertory management; copyright; recording arts; computer and electronic music

- Developing and practicing music therapy
- Programming and publishing musical works

  designing or serving as artistic director of festivals, summer programs, concert series, workshops, master classes, seminars

- Exhibiting, programming, and publishing explanations, studies, and critiques; research and scholarly findings; translations and compilations

  books and chapters in books; articles, monographs; delivering or publishing conference papers, panel discussions, proceedings; lectures; critical editions of music; reviews of books, musical works, and performances or productions; appointments as artist-in-residence; performances as part of professional meetings; workshops; master classes; interviews; seminars; computer applications; program notes

Service

The utilization of disciplinary and other expertise to support and advance the institution, music, and the community. Each faculty member undertakes a judicious single or multiple selection among the following:

Assisting the Institution

- Organizing, coordinating, administering, or maintaining curricular programs, academic departments, campus organizations, technical facilities, conferences and other institutional events
- Serving on committees
- Identifying and writing grant proposals; fund raising
- Recruiting students and faculty
- Appraising institutional and departmental results in light of goals and objectives
- Providing expertise that assists the work of other institutional units, including libraries, academic and administrative departments, development offices, and support agencies

Advancing the Profession Beyond the Institution

- Organizing, coordinating, or administering exhibitions, performances, projects, organizations, or events
- Professional writing
- Editing
- Serving on committees, task forces, review and advisory boards, councils
- Adjudicating and reviewing
- Consulting

Contributing to the Community

▶ Participating in working groups, boards, arts councils, and community events

▶ Consulting, clinical work, and practice in the community

▶ Contributing to public education through teaching, performances, presentations, and consulting

THE WORK OF THE THEATRE FACULTY

The following outline** [see previous note] presents a composite list of responsibilities undertaken by theatre faculty. Users should note the following:

▶ **The excitement, power, and achievement of great teaching, creative work-research, and service come from individual expertise, inspiration, and involvement, and from institutional support. This document can only note these possibilities; realizing them is an individual and local matter.**

▶ **Users may wish to rearrange the outline or double list categories such as administration, grant writing, adjudication, consulting, etc., to better fit their mission, goals, and objectives.**

▶ **This document assumes a commitment to introduce students to works and techniques from various world cultures and historical periods.**

Users of the outline may obtain a more comprehensive picture by considering these activities in relation to various approaches and perspectives for content outlined in Section II.

***Italics* are used to indicate a few primary examples in each category.**

Teaching

The combination of content, intellectual processes, approaches, and preparations that produce instruction and associated services for students at the institution. Each faculty member undertakes a judicious selection of the following:

Delivering Group or Individual Instruction That Enables Students to

▶ Create Theatre

— develop knowledge and skills in the practice of theatre arts and theatre-related disciplines

acting; speech; voice; movement; directing; interpretation; stage, costume, sound and lighting design; technical operations; film/video production; computer technologies; participation in collaborative projects

— integrate and synthesize knowledge and skills in the creation or performance of works for the theatre

playwriting; translation of foreign dramatic literature; improvisation; preparing and presenting theatrical works; dramaturgy

▶ Study, Understand, and Evaluate Theatre, Its Influences, and Its Relationships

— analyze how works of theatre function as artistic and aesthetic entities

dramatic theory; play analysis

— understand the history of the theatre, including the impact of specific works on the discipline itself

repertory; historical description and analysis; bibliography; textual criticism and editing; style; performance practices; ethnology; evolution of theatrical technique

— analyze past and present relationships of theatre with events, ideas, people, and situations as studied through the methodologies and theories of the humanities, social sciences, and natural sciences

aesthetics; sociology of theatre; psychology of theatre; theatre criticism; philosophy of theatre; acoustics and theatre architecture; drama therapy; relationships to general history

▶ Teach Theatre

— integrate and synthesize knowledge, skills, and technologies in the development and delivery of instruction

teaching skills; educational methodologies; evaluation; course and curriculum content and development; instructional innovation; research; development and preparation of instructional materials; organizational and management skills; advising; academic and career counseling; philosophical, sociological, and historical connections between theatre and education

▶ Apply and Present Theatre and Facilitate Theatre Activities

— practice in fields involving connections between theatre and such areas as administration, commerce, public relations, therapies, and technologies

administration of presenting organizations and venues; artist management; drama therapy; media arts; community service

These aspects of teaching are delivered through individual and group instruction; tutorials; directed research; field trips and attendance at off-campus performances; preparation for and presentation of theatrical performances; master classes; seminars; student teaching; and in informal settings.

Preparing for Studio, Performance, or Class Instruction

▶ Maintaining artistic and intellectual currency in the discipline
> *creative work and research; independent, individual, or group study; professional exchange; successful participation in collaborative projects*

▶ Creating, discovering, integrating, synthesizing, and applying ideas, subject matter, and technique for specific instructional applications
> *course and project development; rehearsal preparation; awareness of ongoing trends, issues, and technologies*

▶ Directing, interpretation, designing, administering, coordinating, and supervising student projects and productions
> *research; auditions; rehearsing; choreographing; technical directing; theses; dissertations; design portfolio development*

Evaluating

▶ Measuring the development of student competence
> *entrance auditions; performances; written projects; examinations; ongoing and exit assessment*

▶ Assessing personal effectiveness
> *studio, classroom, individual, and informal teaching*

▶ Appraising course and student project results in light of goals and objectives
> *course and curricula review; critique of methodology*

Advising

▶ Advising students regarding curricula and projects
▶ Providing guidance and direction in the field
▶ Mentoring students toward professionalism in practice and/or teaching in the discipline

Creative Work and Research

The combination of individual work in theatre and its presentation in exhibitions, performances, productions, and publications in various formats. Each faculty member undertakes a judicious single or multiple selection among the following:

Creating Theatre

▶ Creating a work of theatre
> *study, research, and synthesis that lead to original works, translations, interpretations, and adaptations (full-length and one-act plays, screenplays, children's theatre, electronic media, interactive applications); contribution and participation as a collaborative artist in the creation of theatre*

▶ Performing a work of theatre

> *study, research, and practice that lead to live, broadcast, or computer performances, films or videos — including acting; directing; stage, costume, and lighting designing; technical directing; dramaturgy*

▶ Developing new technologies, techniques, and approaches that advance creative capabilities in theatre

Studying Theatre and Its Influences

▶ Analyzing how works of theatre function

> *dramatic theory, criticism, interpretation*

▶ Investigating and understanding the history and impact of theatre

> *repertory; studies and analyses from historical, geographical, cultural, religious, and other perspectives; history of ideas in theatre; performance practices; bibliography; textual criticism and editing*

▶ Researching the physiological and psychological impact of theatre

> *perception of theatrical phenomena; relationship of theatre to various specialized audiences; therapeutic applications; theatre as a laboratory for research in human psychophysiology; the biology of performance*

▶ Exploring the sociological impact of theatre

> *theatre and the human condition; theatre and society; ethnographic and demographic studies; marketing*

▶ Creating and assessing ideas and values about theatre

> *aesthetics, criticism, and philosophy of theatre*

▶ Investigating and understanding issues and developments in theatre design, technology, and engineering

▶ Considering the multiple influences on theatre from various sources

> *conditions, events, ideas, and technologies*

▶ Integrating and synthesizing some or all of the above

Advancing the Pedagogy of Theatre

▶ Developing instructional materials, curricula, and technologies that have broad impact on the field

▶ Determining causes and effects in educational settings

▶ Integrating and applying theoretical and practical knowledge in educational policy settings

▶ Exploring philosophical, sociological, and historical connections between theatre and education

Applying Theatre and Facilitating Theatre Activities

▶ Exploring and developing connections between theatre and such areas as administration, commerce, public relations, therapies, and technologies

administration of presenting organizations and venues; artist and repertory management; theatre-related industries; copyright; media arts

▶ Developing and practicing drama therapy

▶ Programming works of theatre

designing or serving as artistic director of festivals; summer programs; theatre series; workshops; master classes; seminars

▶ Exhibiting, programming, and publishing explanations, studies, and critiques; research and scholarly findings; translations and compilations

books and chapters in books; articles, monographs; delivering or publishing conference papers, panel discussions, proceedings; lectures; reviews of books, performances, productions, or new works of theatre; appointments as artist-in-residence; performances as part of professional meetings; workshops; master classes; interviews; seminars; computer applications; program notes; exhibitions of stage and historical costume, stage designs, etc.

Service

The utilization of disciplinary and other expertise to support and advance the institution, the theatre profession, and the community. Each faculty member undertakes a judicious single or multiple selection among the following:

Assisting the Institution

▶ Organizing, coordinating, administering, or maintaining curricular programs, academic departments, campus organizations, technical facilities, or institutional events

▶ Serving on committees

▶ Identifying and writing grant proposals; fund raising

▶ Recruiting students and faculty

▶ Appraising institutional and departmental results in light of mission, goals, and objectives

▶ Providing expertise that assists the work of other institutional units, including libraries, special collections, academic and administrative departments, development offices, and support agencies

Advancing the Profession Beyond the Institution

▶ Organizing, coordinating, or administering exhibitions, performances, projects, organizations, or events

▶ Professional writing

▶ Editing — journals, newsletters, etc.

▶ Serving on committees, task forces, review and advisory boards, councils

▶ Adjudicating and reviewing, peer evaluations

▶ Consulting

Contributing to the Community

▶ Participating in working groups, boards, arts councils, performance organizations, and community events

▶ Consulting, clinical work, and practice in the community

▶ Contributing to public education through teaching, performances, and presentations

VI. CONCLUSION

As the work of the arts faculty continues to evolve, new combinations of elements, approaches, and perspectives will be formed. The ability to distinguish between fads and trends and to place analyses and decisions in the contexts of mission, goals, objectives, and priorities is critical to the future of each arts unit, to the overall productivity of each institution of higher education, and to the progress of cultural development within and beyond the institution. As this document has shown, the arts disciplines represent a large field filled with various needs, responsibilities, issues, and opportunities. Each institution with arts-related goals will choose to focus its work on one or more aspects of the field. When such choices are made, many parameters of faculty work and faculty evaluation begin to arrange themselves and to establish certain internal goals, objectives, and priorities. However, each institution is responsible for going beyond this natural progression. Each must determine how it will develop and employ personnel resources to fulfill aspirations on many levels.

The arts in American higher education are one of the glories of our nation's cultural life. A premise underlying the integration of the arts throughout our higher education system is that work in the arts and work about the arts are interdependent, that both gain from strong interrelationships, that scholarship and artistry support each other on many levels, including the scholarly and artistic work of specific individuals. The successes of the past challenge us to continue our efforts, and thus to ensure the productive continuation of these important linkages. The work of the faculty can only be regarded as a central element in higher education. Therefore, it is important that arts faculty and administrators take first responsibility to clarify and present their values and positions as the basis for developing a greater understanding of the work of arts faculties in specific institutions and throughout higher education as a whole. This document marks the beginning of a new level of effort in this regard. The real effect, however, will come from the aggregate impact of reconsideration and possible revision of institutional approaches throughout the nation.

VII. ACKNOWLEDGEMENTS

The cooperation and support of all institutions and individuals holding memberships in the sponsoring and consultant organizations were essential to the development of this project.

Special appreciation is extended to Syracuse University, and Assistant Vice Chancellor Robert Diamond, for convening the national project to expand definitions of scholarship in American higher education. Syracuse was the first among equals in a consortium of seven institutions, each of which contributed to a project on the importance of undergraduate teaching. This present project emerged from these efforts.

The Interdisciplinary Task Force that developed the initial draft and reviewed subsequent drafts made the project credible in content and pleasurable in its development. Members of the Task Force are identified on the following page.

Meetings of the Task Force were funded by sponsoring and consultant organizations — Landscape Architectural Accreditation Board, National Architectural Accrediting Board, National Association of Schools of Art and Design, National Association of Schools of Dance, National Association of Schools of Music, National Association of Schools of Theatre, and University Film and Video Association; and the following institutions in the parent project consortium — Carnegie Mellon University, The Ohio State University, Syracuse University, University of Massachusetts, and University of Michigan. The Lilly Endowment and the Fund for the Improvement of Secondary Education also provided partial support for Task Force activity.

Special appreciation is expressed to the staff members of the sponsoring organizations. Willa Shaffer of the National Office for Arts Accreditation in Higher Education prepared various drafts and the final text for publication. Samuel Hope and Catherine Sentman were the principal compilers of the general text.

A final word of appreciation is forwarded to the hundreds of individual administrators and faculty members who participated at various stages of text development. Without their dedicated efforts, neither this document nor the work of arts faculties in higher education would be possible.

MEMBERS OF THE INTERDISCIPLINARY TASK FORCE

Co-Chairs:
Donald M. Lantzy, Dean, College of Visual and Performing Arts, Syracuse University
Bruce Abbey, Dean, School of Architecture, Syracuse University
Architecture
Robert M. Beckley, FAIA, Dean, College of Architecture and Urban Planning, University of Michigan
Marvin Malecha, AIA, Dean, College of Environmental Design, California State Polytechnic
Art and Design
Robert Arnold, Associate Provost for Curriculum and Instruction, The Ohio State University
Larry Walker, Director, School of Art and Design, Georgia State University
Dance
Nancy Smith Fichter, Chairperson, Department of Dance, Florida State University
Ann Wagner, Chair, Department of Dance, Saint Olaf College
Film and Video
Ben Levin, Department of Radio, Television, and Film, University of North Texas
Landscape Architecture
Sally Schauman, FASLA, Chair, Department of Landscape Architecture, University of Washington
Mark Lindhult, ASLA, Department of Landscape Architecture and Regional Planning, University of Massachusetts
Music
Marilyn Taft Thomas, Head, Department of Music, Carnegie Mellon University
Kenneth A. Keeling, Head, Department of Music, University of Tennessee
Theatre
James L. Steffensen, Chair, Department of Drama, Dartmouth College
Carole W. Singleton, Department of Theatre Arts, Howard University

Staff:

Samuel Hope, Executive Director, National Office for Arts Accreditation in Higher Education

John M. Maudlin-Jeronimo, Executive Director, National Architectural Accrediting Board

Karen P. Moynahan, Associate Director, National Office for Arts Accreditation in Higher Education

Karen L. Niles, Staff Vice President, Planning and Programs, Landscape Architectural Accreditation Board

Catherine Sentman, Projects Consultant, National Office for Arts Accreditation in Higher Education   □

American Assembly of Collegiate Schools of Business

DEFINING SCHOLARLY WORK
IN MANAGEMENT EDUCATION*

Report/July 1992

by William K. Laidlaw, Jr.
Executive Vice President, American Assembly of Collegiate Schools of Business

BACKGROUND

In most universities and colleges in the United States, faculty promotion and tenure decisions are based on criteria involving research, teaching and service. Depending upon the historical roots and thrust of the institution, the weights assigned to these criteria often vary. Ernest Boyer of the Carnegie Foundation for the Advancement of Teaching argues, in his book *Scholarship Reconsidered: Priorities for the Professoriate* (1990), that "a wide gap now exists between the myth and the reality of academic life. Almost all colleges pay lip service to the trilogy of teaching, research, and service, but when it comes to making judgments about professional performance, the three rarely are assigned to equal merit . . . the time has come to move beyond the tired, old 'teaching versus research' debate and give the familiar and honorable term 'scholarship' a broader, more capacious meaning, one that brings legitimacy to the full scope of academic work."

Some stimulation for our involvement in the project came from an essay by Eugene Rice, Antioch College entitled "The New American Scholar: Scholarship and the Purposes of the University." Rice suggests a four-part definition of scholarship to replace the usual three-part approach of research, teaching, and service. Drawing on the work of Ernest Boyer, Ernest Lynton, Lee Shulman, and others, Rice breaks scholarship down into four distinct yet interrelated components:

1. The Scholarship of Discovery.
    The advancement of knowledge — essentially original research.
2. The Scholarship of Integration.
    The integration of knowledge — synthesizing and reintegrating knowledge, revealing

    * Reprinted with the permission of the American Assembly of Collegiate Schools of Business, 605 Old Ballas Road, Suite 220, St. Louis, MO 63141-7077; 314/872-8481; fax 314/872-8495. AACSB gives special thanks to the Richard D. Irwin, Inc., for partial funding in support of its effort.

new patterns of meaning and new relationships between the parts and the whole. Reaching across disciplinary boundaries to pull disparate views and information together in creative ways, i.e., to synthesize, to look for new relationships between the parts and the whole, to relate the past and future to the present, and to fetter out patterns of meaning that cannot be seen through traditional disciplinary lenses.

3. The Scholarship of Practice.

The application of knowledge — directly related to an individual's scholarly specialization. Professional service that is based on and requires a scholarly background in the discipline.

4. The Scholarship of Teaching.

The transformation of knowledge through teaching — including pedagogical content knowledge and discipline-specific educational theory.

Rice concludes: "We know that what is being proposed challenges a hierarchical arrangement of monumental proportions — a status system that is firmly fixed in the consciousness of the present faculty and the academy's organizational policies practices. What is being called for is a broader, more open field where these different forms of scholarship can interact, inform, and enrich one another, and faculty can follow their interests, build on their strengths, and be rewarded for what they spend most of their scholarly energy doing. All faculty ought to be scholars in this broader sense, deepening their preferred approaches to knowing but constantly pressing, and being pressed by peers, to enlarge their scholarly capacities and encompass other — often contrary — ways of thinking." (p. 6)

There is nothing discipline-specific about the relative importance of these criteria as they relate to the evaluation of academic work. Rather, the debate about their importance embraces all of higher education, especially today, when there is considerable criticism from the public and other professions that research receives too much of the emphasis. The situation in management education is no different, and if one looks at the roots of the problem, the current situation is understandable. In the late 1950s and early 1960s, major reports on the field of management education were sponsored by the Ford and Carnegie Foundations. Among the findings of those reports were that business schools were too vocational, lacked academic rigor, and taught subjects that were not founded in basic research. The Ford Foundation followed up its report with an investment of more than $30 million to upgrade the quality of doctoral programs, to incorporate research capability from other disciplines, and to create an environment that valued research as the basis for the development of the disciplines in management education. Our field has spent the last 30 years seeking academic respectability among university colleagues by emphasizing research and scholarship, often narrowly defined. Now the difficulty we face is that the reward system is at odds with the demands from at least part of our customer market. To be sure, our multi-disciplinary field continues to value pure research in order to advance the streams of knowledge. But not all faculty, and not all institutions, care to or are qualified to conduct that type of research. Other definitions of "research" are needed in order to interpret pure research to classroom use and to apply the research in practice.

In January 1987, the Final Report of the AACSB Task Force on Faculty Research defined research in the following way: "Research must be written, be subject to scrutiny and criticism by one's peers and extend the boundaries of current knowledge." The committee went on to provide categories of research to fit the definition:

1. *Theoretical or empirical "discovery" research, including integrative and interdisciplinary research which makes new discoveries by linking avenues of thought across diverse disciplines.*

2. *Applied research in which one applies other's discovery research to new context, fields, industries, firms, nations, time periods, etc.*

3. *Written teaching cases accompanied by an instructor's manual which can be scrutinized and critiqued by one's peers.*

4. *Computer software which is circulated and not totally proprietary.*

5. *Textbooks and other pedagogical writing which extend the boundaries of knowledge, circulate and can be critiqued.*

    Written material (such as some consulting reports) that is proprietary would not meet the definition and thus would not qualify as research. Written cases without a published instructor's manual would also not qualify. Such material lacks the necessary ingredients of scrutiny by one's peers and of allowing public determination of how the research extends the boundaries of current knowledge.

    We are not implying that all business schools should encourage or reward all five types of research listed. Indeed, it is proper that some schools will choose to reward or pursue only a subset of these types, depending on clienteles they serve. Thus, some schools may choose an emphasis on discovery research at the expense of encouraging textbooks and case writing; others may legitimately do the reverse. In fact, Schools which need to revive their faculty research activities ought to consider that legitimate research, as we have defined it, includes translating other people's discovery research into a form that makes it applicable to practitioners. There is no presumption here that only discovery research counts or is appropriate. Rather, we suggest only that every AACSB-accredited school incorporate in its standards for tenure and promotion a requirement that faculty member[s] engage in at least one of these five types of research.

In April, 1991, the AACSB membership approved new standards of accreditation which require that a "formal, periodic review process should exist for reappointment, promotion, and tenure decisions that produces results consistent with the school's mission and objectives." The standards point out that among the "criteria used for evaluation, attention should be given to course development, effective teaching, and instructional innovations." (pp. 12 & 13) Another standard calls for the school to "support continuing faculty intellectual development and renewal." (p. 13) The standard on "Intellectual Contributions" requires "faculty members (to) make intellectual contributions on a continuing basis appropriate to the mission of the school. The outputs of intellectual contributions should be available for public scrutiny by academic peers or practitioners." (p. 31)

The standard goes on to interpret the components of intellectual contributions as the creation of new knowledge (basic scholarship); the application, transfer, and interpretation of knowledge to improve management practice and teaching (applied scholarship); and the enhancement of the educational value of instructional efforts of the institution or discipline (instructional developments).

As a result of the work of The Accreditation Project committee, and following upon the work of Porter & McKibbin entitled *Management Education and Development: Drift or Thrust into the 21st Century?* the AACSB leadership felt it important to conduct an inquiry into the nature of Ph.D. programs. Since those programs are such an important factor in developing not only knowledge and research skills, but also in establishing the basic value system of faculty members, it seemed logical that major reform in management education would not take place unless it started with the products of the doctoral programs. Of particular interest was the preparation for teaching offered by doctoral programs and the relative importance between teaching and research implied by the values imparted in Ph.D. programs.

THE CURRENT PROJECT

In the fall of 1991, the AACSB Board of Directors agreed to participate in a project entitled "Defining Scholarly Work" of national scope which is coordinated by Syracuse

University with support from the Fund for the Improvement for Postsecondary Education (FIPSE) and the Lilly Endowment. The project focuses on enhancing the status of teaching within the faculty reward system and, ultimately, looking at opportunities for changing the promotion/tenure and merit systems. Eighteen academic/professional associations are participating in this project. The Lilly Project demonstrated that all groups of faculty and administrators desire a balanced integration of research and teaching. The perception, however, is that the next group higher in the academic hierarchy places greater value on research. Perceptions, then, appear to be a major barrier to changing policies for evaluating faculty performance.

Data available from the Lilly study show that differences exist by discipline within the business schools. For example, economics, marketing, and finance faculty would like to see more emphasis placed on research while management, MIS, and accounting faculty would like to see the emphasis moved more towards teaching. Recognizing that differences between disciplines are important, and that the missions of different schools create significantly different environments for evaluating research and teaching, the AACSB Board agreed to participate in the next stage of this effort, which was to convene a task force during April 1992 to determine how best to evaluate the portfolios of activities faculty members may present as evidence that they engage in various kind[s] of scholarship and teaching activities.

The Assembly agreed to participate in the Syracuse/Lilly Project for several reasons:

1. Not all of the problems associated with faculty rewards systems are discipline-specific. Hence, individual disciplines and their associations may be a good place to start, but they cannot be expected to bring about reform single-handedly. Similar initiatives must be launched within higher education associations and college and university administrations if there is to be any substantial change.

2. AACSB's role should not be to prescribe a certain formula, but rather to suggest alternative ways in which schools of business may address this issue. Any statement from the Assembly must be adaptable to the varied needs of different departments and institutions.

3. Reform efforts should focus on increasing flexibility within this system.

4. The faculty reward system is flawed, but it is not clear how.

5. There must be a "product" as a result of faculty work that must be replicable and available for external evaluation.

A task force was formed consisting of representatives from six of the schools involved in an earlier phase of the Lilly project, as well as individuals with significant experience in the new formulation of standards and procedures for AACSB accreditation. Its members are:

  Alutto, Joseph — Dean, The Ohio State University

  Burman, George — Dean, Syracuse University

  Epple, Dennis — Ph.D., Carnegie Mellon University

  Goodridge, Lyn — Dean, University of New Hampshire

  Hasler, William — Dean, University of California at Berkeley

  Jones, Barbara — Dean, Prairie View A&M University

  Miller, Edwin — Ph.D., The University of Michigan

  O'Brien, Thomas — Dean, The University of Massachusetts-Amherst

  Sheftall, Willis — Dean, Morehouse College

In addition, Mr. William Setten represented Richard D. Irwin, Inc., who has made funds available to help meet some of the costs associated with this project. Joining from the AACSB staff were Milton Blood, Director of Accreditation, and William K. Laidlaw, Jr., Executive Vice President. Finally, Robert Diamond, Assistant Vice Chancellor of the Center for Instructional Development at Syracuse University, and Director of the Lilly Project, facilitated the meeting.

Charged with redefining scholarship in order to incorporate aspects into teaching and service activities, the task force produced the following definitions supplemented by examples. The committee used as its basis the interpretations for intellectual contributions from Section I, item C.1 of the new accreditation standards:

▶ Basic scholarship: The creation of new knowledge.

  Outputs from basic scholarship activities include publication and refereed journals, research monographs, scholarly books, chapters in scholarly books, proceedings from scholarly meetings, papers presented at academic meetings, publicly available research working papers, and papers presented at faculty research seminars. Discovery research, the testing of theories, is included along with developing theories based on case development. Interdisciplinary work across fields, e.g., environmental studies and management, or language studies and international business, are also included.

▶ Applied scholarship: The application, transfer, and interpretation of knowledge to approved management practice and teaching.

  Outputs from applied/service scholarship activities include publication and professional journals, professional presentations, public/trade/practitioner journals, in-house book reviews, and papers presented at faculty workshops. Also included are case writing to illustrate existing theories, adapting pure research of others into text, service to community (e.g., internships and case enrichment), interpreting real world experience to classroom use that is generalizable and reusable, and interdisciplinary work across fields such as environmental studies in management or language studies and international business.

▶ Instructional Development: The enhancement of the educational value of instructional efforts of the institution or discipline.

Output from instructional development activities include textbooks, publications and pedagogical journals, written cases with instructional materials, instructional software, and publicly available materials describing the design and implementation of new courses. Also included are executive education course teaching, internships supervised by faculty, and materials used to enhance student learning, e.g., for advising and mentoring students and for assessment. In addition, developing new curriculum materials or support materials to be used by others (slides, video presentations, computer software, teachers' manuals) are included.

The following additional observations were made by task force members. Because management education is multi-disciplinary in nature and because the accreditation standards are now mission-driven, there is a need for a range of options for schools. The fact that different institutions have different values necessitates varied approaches to evaluation. Such evaluations should relate to accreditation, faculty development, and continuous improvement. It is important to avoid putting a system in place that would lead to stagnation.

For true change to be made, faculty must play a dominate role. And decisions would be better if they were program-based, rather than simply discipline-based.

A list of indicators or options of scholarship might be used to challenge colleges to select a set consistent with their mission and then demonstrate how they meet those indicators.

HOW THIS REPORT WILL BE USED

As part of the implementation phase of the new accreditation standards, AACSB is producing a Handbook (loose-leaf) and considerable printed materials to guide accreditors and schools in implementing the new system. The Handbook will include interpretive statements designed to help accreditation visiting teams and committees, as well as schools and the staff, understand the intent of the standards. It is envisioned that a two-to-three page excerpt of this document would be prepared as an interpretive guide on scholarly activity to be included in the Handbook. In that way it will directly impact the 280+ accredited schools plus the 100-200 more intending to apply for accreditation. □

Association for Education in Journalism and Mass Communication

REPORT OF THE ASSOCIATION FOR EDUCATION IN JOURNALISM & MASS COMMUNICATION ON THE DEFINITION OF SCHOLARSHIP IN JOURNALISM*

November 19, 1992

Task Force: Sharon Brock, Ohio State; Marilyn Kern-Foxworth, Texas A&M; Ralph Lowenstein, University of Florida; Will Norton, University of Nebraska at Lincoln; Lana Rakow, University of Wisconsin-Parkside; Carol Reuss, University of North Carolina at Chapel Hill; David Rubin, Syracuse University; Ardyth Sohn, University of Colorado; Robert Wicks, Indiana University; Lee Wilkins, University of Missouri-Columbia.

INTRODUCTION

Almost all universities list "teaching, service, and research" as the three primary criteria on which tenure, promotion, and merit pay will be based. Yet the three criteria are rarely given equal weight in the deliberative process. To explore how these criteria should be redefined for faculty in journalism and mass communication, the Association for Education in Journalism and Mass Communication participated in a national project conducted by Syracuse University under a grant from the Lilly Endowment. The project brought together many academic disciplines, ranging from geography to history, and explored the expanding range of activities that qualify as scholarly or creative research. Representatives from AEJMC met separately, as part of the project and composed a statement on the discipline-specific varieties of scholarship and creative activity in journalism and mass communication. They hoped that this statement could become a productive guide for departments and colleges of journalism and mass communication, and for the university committees and administrations that ultimately make the decisions about tenure, promotion and merit pay. AEJMC recognizes that each university has its own traditions and emphases, and distributes this statement as one that provides parameters and choices, rather than prescriptions.

---

* Reprinted with the permission of the Association for Education in Journalism and Mass Communication.

STATEMENT

Journalism education in North America is less than 100 years old. As an academic field it grew out of the newspaper professions and gradually evolved to incorporate other disciplines related to the mass media, including advertising, radio, television, and public relations. From the beginning, this new discipline depended upon a regular infusion of teaching talent from other disciplines and the non-academic professions to which it was related.

Although holders of Ph.D.'s are now more common in the teaching ranks of schools and departments of journalism and mass communication, the average faculty includes a mix of teachers with long professional experience and teachers with heavier research qualifications. Both are absolutely necessary for the diversity of the faculty, for the optimum enhancement of student knowledge, and for the support and respect necessary from both academia and the professions.

The mission of schools and departments of journalism and mass communication must embrace both academic and professional work. Faculty members or their programs are expected to contribute to the advancement of the academic or professional fields through scholarly or creative work, or both.

Such contributions may take a variety of forms; both are conducted within specific realms of knowledge reflecting academic and/or professional expertise. Scholarship and creative work address specific problems, using methodologies appropriate to those problems. In the field of mass communication, these methodologies may include qualitative, quantitative, legal, and historical.

Continuing scholarship or creative production is an essential part of the academic environment. Those faculty who do not actively conduct research or engage in creative activity will, in the long run, be less able to teach effectively, except in the relatively small portion of the curriculum that remains virtually unchanged over time.

The standards for judging excellence vary, and faculty members' work will be evaluated by people with national reputations in the relevant areas of scholarship or creative work.

University administrations must consider this unique mix necessary for a strong journalism and mass communication program when considering scholarship and creative activity in relation to tenure, promotion, and merit pay.

QUALITIES OF SCHOLARLY/CREATIVE WORK

Among the qualities to be considered in evaluating scholarship and/or creative work are:

- ▶ originality of the work
- ▶ actual or likely impact of the work
- ▶ contribution to theory
- ▶ contribution to practice
- ▶ thoroughness of analysis
- ▶ scope, depth, and significance of subjects covered
- ▶ clarity of expression
- ▶ reputation and selectivity of the forum in which it is presented

The publication or public presentation of scholarship and creative work may occur in a variety of forms, and may involve dissemination to fellow scholars, professional audiences, and the general public.

FORMS OF SCHOLARLY/CREATIVE WORK

Among specific forms of scholarship and creative work to be considered appropriate are:

1. Scholarly books and textbooks
2. Peer-reviewed and invited chapters in books
3. Peer-reviewed and invited journal articles
4. Other articles that advance knowledge in the field
5. Other works in professional and consumer publications if they demonstrate high standards of professional practice
6. Invited and peer-reviewed monographs
7. Published proceedings of scholarly or professional presentations
8. Book review
9. Editorships of scholarly material
10. Reviewed electronic or film production in which the individual exhibits principal creative control and which contributes to scholarly knowledge or demonstrates superior professional performance
11. Peer-evaluated exhibitions or collections
12. Invited or peer-reviewed photographic or graphic design publication or exhibition

13. Peer-reviewed and invited scholarly papers
14. Mass media-related software patented, widely accepted, or peer reviewed

The weight given to each of these factors might vary between journalism and mass communication programs. Since no two journalism and mass communication curriculums are alike, schools and departments that offer specialized programs might add other research and creative activity that will have equal validity to those named above. ☐

Council of Administrators of Family and Consumer Sciences

RECOGNITION AND REWARDS IN THE FAMILY AND CONSUMER SCIENCES*

INTRODUCTION

by E. Audrey Clark

Higher education appears to be standing at the threshold of significant reform. One aspect of impending change is the recurrent challenge of prominent educators to improve undergraduate teaching and provide services to the communities in which institutions are located (Boyer, 1990; Rice, 1991). Additionally, many educators believe that universities and colleges place too much emphasis on research and that the focus of faculty work should be broadened to include other scholarly activities.

Refocusing the definition of scholarship should be beneficial to disciplines such as Family and Consumer Sciences, where faculty have diverse and often nontraditional assignments. Our discipline is applied, requiring many faculty to be involved in "hands-on" instruction or service anchored to community projects. Instead of library or laboratory research, the assignments of faculty often encompass activities such as leading discussion groups, developing curriculum, coordinating internships, administering programs and supervising student teaching.

Although diversity in faculty assignments may enhance undergraduate teaching and community involvement and should position participants at the cutting edge of educational practice, this is not always the case. Some experts suggest that "service, teaching and creativity are risky priorities for faculty seeking promotion and tenure" (Diamond, 1993). Boyer (1990) argued that almost all colleges claim allegiance to teaching, research, and service, but rarely assign equal merit to the three when making judgments about professional performance. Even when teaching is identified as the most important mission of an institution, faculty commonly perceive that retention, tenure and promotion committees discount its value in comparison to research and publication (Gray, Froh & Diamond, 1992).

---

* Reprinted with the permission of the Council of Administrators of Family and Consumer Sciences. Copies of this report can be obtained by writing: Family Environmental Sciences, California State University Northridge, 18111 Nordhoff Street, Northridge, CA 91330-8308; 818/885-3051; fax 818/885-4778.

The Council of Administrators of Family and Consumer Sciences (CAFCS) entered a formal dialogue concerning these issues in 1991. At that time, the Association agreed to participate in an initiative conducted by the Center for Instructional Development (CID) at Syracuse University. The initiative was supported by the Fund for the Improvement of Post Secondary Education and the Lilly Endowment. It has addressed changing the priorities within universities and the associated issue of faculty recognition and rewards.

A CAFCS task force met in early 1992 to consider broadening the definition of scholarship within Family and Consumer Sciences. The group identified aspects of faculty work that it felt could be considered scholarly but may not be recognized and rewarded appropriately within universities. The composition and findings of the task force appear in Appendix A.

The findings of the Task Force were summarized in the National Council of Administrators of Home Economics *Newsletter* (March, 1992). Additional discussions were held at two subsequent annual conferences. The second of these was reported in the Council of Administrators of Family and Consumer Sciences *Newsletter* (May, 1994).

The ideas evolving from these meetings are presented here for your further consideration. The dialogue continues, and the Association seeks your input and refinement of the concepts presented in this document.

PART ONE
RECOGNITION AND REWARDS
by E. Audrey Clark

Faculty Role
Guideline: *Faculty should engage in scholarship throughout their careers. Ongoing scholarship is essential for faculty to maintain currency, to communicate course content effectively to students in undergraduate and graduate programs, and to participate in the higher learning community.*

In order to remain vital as educators, all faculty — not just traditional research faculty — need to involve themselves in scholarly activity. Even faculty who are assigned entirely to classroom teaching must constantly re-evaluate curricula in the light of emerging knowledge, seek new ways to deliver educational messages, and adjust their presentations to new and diverse student groups in order to remain at the cutting edge of the field. This work is different from laboratory research, but is scholarly in its own right. Similarly, the academic who formulates new knowledge as the result of community involvement is engaging in scholarly activity, which in turn, may enhance the classroom experience of students.

It is only through continuing scholarship that expertise develops. Expertise that emerges during student days should be nourished during early faculty careers. Although the focus of study may change over time, scholarship should continue to strengthen through the years. The mature scholar contributes to the discipline by adding to the store of knowledge and serving as a role model or mentor to the next generation of scholars.

Guideline: *Scholarship can take many forms.*

Traditionally, scholarship has been narrowly defined in higher education as studies that use the scientific method. The Task Force of 1992 agreed with Boyer (1990) that there is a need to broaden the definition of scholarship. Producing qualitative research, writing articles for lay publications, developing curricula, and engaging in classroom research were cited by the Task Force as examples of activities appropriate for the attention of Family and Consumer Science scholars.

The scholarly process is often as important as the scholarly product. Lynton (1992) characterized the scholarly process as reasoned, reflective and instructive to the scholar as well as the learner. Examination of the scholarly process, as well as product, facilitates evaluation of works-in-progress. Obtaining final research results may require investment of extended periods of time, a daunting reality for faculty subject to time-sensitive decisions such as award of tenure. Process evaluation can ameliorate such a condition, providing feedback along the way.

Scholarship may be enhanced through collaboration with colleagues and other agencies such as interdisciplinary groups and coalitions. The interaction among professionals with different experiential and academic backgrounds can generate creative solutions to problems and innovative directions for research.

Guideline: *Teaching, as a form of scholarship, is a primary responsibility of all faculty, often extending beyond the classroom.*

Teaching is a primary responsibility of faculty at all colleges and universities. The scholarship of teaching involves more than presenting the same lecture to generations of students. It requires working at the cutting edge of the discipline: keeping current with advances in the discipline and exploring teaching methods that make the subject matter relevant to students.

Curriculum development, academic advisement of a developmental nature, preparing materials for classroom use, mentoring graduate students, and many other aspects of faculty work fall under the rubric of teaching. These should be recognized and rewarded appropriately.

Guideline: *In order to be recognized and rewarded within the university context, scholarship must be compatible with departmental and institutional missions.*

Scholarly work can address many agendas: not all are appropriate to pursue within an employing institution. Institutions and departments differ in their scholarly emphases. Given this diversity of mission, it is unlikely that a single academic unit will address all of the goals of a discipline. A disunity may exist between disciplinary and institutional interests. Scholars need to be mindful of the mission under which they are working.

Some scholars may engage in work that does not address disciplinary or institutional priorities. Rice (1993) recommended that faculty should make a distinction between personal scholarly interests and the interests of their employing colleges and universities. He noted that academic freedom does not imply endorsement of personal pursuits on company time, even if the activities are meritorious in themselves. He admonished that faculty need to share the collective responsibilities of their institutions as defined by the institutional mission and goals.

Guideline: *Scholarship must be presented in a form that can be shared, preserved, and evaluated.*

In order to be recognized as scholarly within a particular discipline, faculty work should be accepted by colleagues for its value to the disciplinary body of knowledge and disseminated to the academic community in publications or other accepted forms of documentation. It is not enough to be a scholar; one must also share and preserve the scholarship.

In the case of nontraditional scholarship, faculty members should make every effort to understand the implications for such work prior to using it as a vehicle for promotion and tenure. Departments should clarify their views toward nontraditional scholarship and communicate these perceptions to all involved.

Guideline: *Not all faculty work is scholarly.*

Faculty work involves many essential activities that may not be scholarly in and of themselves. The Task Force of 1992 suggested that activities such as membership on governance committees or search committees is normally a matter of good university citizenship, but rarely a matter of scholarly endeavor.

Institutional Role

Guideline: *Each disciplinary unit (i.e. college, school, department, option), together with the institution, should set parameters for scholarly activity that are consistent* *with the missions of all units involved.*

At the discipline level, administrators and faculty have a special responsibility to guarantee that the mission and goals of the unit are consistent and supportive of the overall institutional mission. Unit mission and goal statements should identify any factors unique to the discipline that need to be recognized in the policies and procedures of the campus as a whole.

Conference participants (Calloway Gardens, 1991) proposed a mission for Family and Consumer Sciences (Home Economics) that has been widely used by faculty and administrators in higher education as a part of strategic planning for departments, schools, and colleges. The mission calls for units to conduct research and provide educational programs that are integrative of its specializations. Further, the mission states that research and educational programs should "focus on the reciprocal relationships among individuals, families, and their near environments." The goal of academic endeavors should be to improve the human condition in a world that is continually changing.

Guideline: *The policies and procedures of the Department, School, and College or University should address all aspects of faculty work that fall within their missions.*

Departments will need to provide definitions of publication and/or service if these are included in the unit mission. This need is particularly evident when forms of publication such as electronic media, exhibitions or trade magazines not traditionally used for academic dissemination are accepted as evidence for promotion and tenure decisions.

Guideline: *The department and institution should evaluate the work of faculty against the faculty assignment rather than against a generic conception of faculty work. Care should be taken to use reliable and valid measures of faculty effectiveness.*

Faculty assignments should be clearly understood from the moment of employment. University units have an obligation to inform potential faculty of the nature of the work that they will be doing. For instance, if faculty are assigned to full-time teaching, they should not be expected to carry a heavy research load. If they are given administrative assignments, they should be evaluated on their competence in that arena.

Some areas of faculty work are difficult to evaluate. Perhaps one of the reasons that traditional research published in refereed journals is entrenched in the faculty reward system is that it is concrete and measurable. Excellent teaching and service contributions may be harder "to get a handle on." For instance, the student evaluation form used as a sole measure of teaching effectiveness may not reflect the true value of instruction. When broadening the scope of scholarship, departments should give careful consideration to developing and implementing appropriate methods to evaluate scholarship.

Role of Professional Organizations

Guideline: *Professional associations should take a lead position in determining the disciplinary agenda. These organizations can be useful in working with colleges, universities, and individual faculty members to identify trends and provide guidance to the academic community.*

Professional associations are well positioned to assist faculty in understanding the requirements of the professions that they represent. Members of these societies establish formal educational requirements, preserve the disciplinary body of knowledge, disseminate research, determine the professional code of ethics, and regulate the fields. The associations have oversight of professional practices and serve as the public voice of their members. These attributes make the organizations important reference points for institutions seeking to understand the unique requirements and educational experiences necessary to move the disciplines forward — experiences that serve as the basis for faculty assignments. Professional organizations can also coordinate communication among campuses regarding progress toward commonly held goals.

Family and Consumer Sciences professional organizations have taken aggressive steps to help define the nature of faculty work. These steps include sponsorship of the Vision Conference at Calloway Gardens (1991) and the Scottsdale Meeting (1993). Outcomes of the Calloway Gardens conference were proposed vision and mission statements for the community of Family and Consumer Science scholars (Appendix B).

At Scottsdale, representatives of five discipline-based organizations developed a conceptual framework for the profession in the 21st Century (Appendix C). The framework includes basic beliefs, planning assumptions, and parameters of professional practice. This framework was endorsed by the Council of Administrators of Family and Consumer Sciences and the American Association of Family and Consumer Sciences in 1994.

The conceptual framework developed at Scottsdale and the mission for the profession in higher education developed at Calloway Gardens are consistent with each other and establish clear reference points for professional objectives for the discipline.

References

Boyer, E. L. (1990). *Scholarship Reconsidered: Priorities for the Professoriate.* Princeton, N. J.: Carnegie Foundation for the Advancement of Teaching.

Diamond, R. M. (1993). How to change the faculty reward system. *AGB Trusteeship*, September/October, 17-21.

Gray, P.; Froh, R. & Diamond, R. (1992). *A National Study of Research Universities on the Balance Between Research and Undergraduate Teaching.* Syracuse, N.Y.: Center for Instructional Development, Syracuse University.

Lynton, E. (1992). Scholarship recognized. Center for Instructional Development Conference at Minnowbrook, N.Y., July 10.

Rice, R. E. (1991). The new American scholar: Scholarship and the purposes of the university. *Metropolitan Universities Journal, 1,* (4), 7-18.

PART TWO
DOCUMENTATION OF FACULTY WORK: FOUR EXAMPLES
by Jerelyn B. Schultz

The potential Achilles heel of the movement to refocus the priorities of the faculty are perceived barriers related to documenting and evaluating faculty work. The reward system will not change unless new ways are found to clearly communicate the significance and quality of faculty efforts.

At the February 1994 annual meeting of the Council of Administrators of Family and Consumer Sciences (CAFCS) held in Greensboro, North Carolina, members had the opportunity to identify ways of documenting faculty work in several non-traditional areas. Presented here are suggested guidelines for documentation of the following activities: fieldwork coordination, curation of an exhibit, director of a child development laboratory and curriculum development for secondary programs. This list does not exhaust the possibilities for evaluating faculty assignments, nor is it meant to be prescriptive. It is intended to stimulate thought regarding the many potential avenues for increasing the array of evaluative evidence needed to document faculty work for Family and Consumer Sciences.

Fieldwork Coordination
Description. This activity involves the placement, coordination, and supervision of students in fieldwork/internship experiences in areas such as hospitality management and fashion merchandising. It requires knowledge of the curriculum, trends in the industry, and the latest research in the field; an understanding of the professional development experiences students should receive; and conducting seminars and teaching courses related to these fieldwork/internship experiences.

Rationale. Fieldwork/internships are a critical link between the university and those industries, organizations/agencies, and schools who hire graduates from family and consumer sciences programs. They provide an opportunity for students to apply what they have learned in the classroom and to bring knowledge gained from the fieldwork/internship experience back to the classroom and the program. These experiences provide simultaneous renewal of the program and strengthen the program's relationships with the external community.

Issues in Documentation. The time, energy, and skills required to do the activity well are not understood by many. Coordinating fieldwork is similar to advising in that it is an activity that often times is not recognized and rewarded. Many underestimate the contribution to the program, department, college, and institution.

Guidelines for Documentation. A portfolio is recommended for documentation of faculty activities related to fieldwork/internship coordination. This portfolio should include a statement of the faculty member's philosophy regarding field work experiences including how they are tied to the curriculum, their role in the professional development of students, and their ability to reflect the latest developments in a particular field. Quantitative indicators include the number of site placements, number of hours spent working with students prior to and following the fieldwork experience, and time spent interacting with supervisors at the sites. Written client feedback should come from both site supervisors and students.

Evidence of student growth/learning during the fieldwork experience and samples of student work during their fieldwork/ internship should be included. A variety of methods can be used for documentation including video tapes, syllabi, and/or materials developed by the faculty member and/or students. The scholarly nature of fieldwork coordination can be represented by providing evidence of the pedagogical impact of fieldwork in a particular field and/or the development of recommendations for curriculum changes.

Presentations can be made at professional meetings and articles/chapters developed to further provide evidence of the scholarly contributions of fieldwork/internship coordination.

Curation of an Exhibit

Description. A faculty member's teaching and scholarly emphasis is in the area of historic textiles and clothing. The department has a nationally known historic costume and textiles collection. This collection is an important vehicle for the department to reach out to the broader community. The collection provides avenues for showcasing historical developments in clothing and textiles and for student research projects. Opportunities exist in many communities and on some campuses to curate an exhibit that includes garments from the collection. Video tapes and/or printed materials that complement the exhibit also can be developed.

Rationale. An exhibit may be the most appropriate vehicle for disseminating the original scholarly work of the faculty member. The research can best be presented in a three dimensional forum that makes it possible for the audience to encounter the garments from the same perspective as the scholar. Although there may be related audio visual materials and publications developed, the core of the scholarship is presented in a way that fully recognizes the nature of the collection from a historical perspective. Care must be taken to emphasize originality in the approach used to create the exhibit, to highlight the role of material culture in society, and to reflect the theory behind material culture studies.

Issues in Documentation. An exhibit might be acceptable within a textiles and clothing department, but not within a human nutrition and food management department. It might be difficult for both the faculty member and the department to document the faculty member's activity in this arena when he or she comes up for promotion and tenure at the college and university levels.

Guidelines for Documentation. Documentation should include a copy of the exhibit script, related publications (catalog, conference papers, etc.), reviews (peer reviews in journals as well as newspaper reviews), and/or video tapes. In order to separate the exhibit from the research that led to the exhibit, the following questions must be addressed: Is the communication aspect of the exhibit equally important and inseparable from the scholarly content? Does the department include other historians who understand and value material culture research and exhibits? Are the faculty member's peers historians or exhibit curators? How do you separate an individual faculty member's contributions from the collaborative efforts of non scholars involved in curating an exhibit?

Director of a Child Development Laboratory

Description. A faculty member is assigned to be the Director of a Child Development Laboratory School. Duties include facilitating faculty and student research, supervising university students who represent a wide spectrum of expertise as they observe/participate in the laboratory program, managing the laboratory (e.g., selecting staff, providing staff development, developing the budget, etc.), representing the laboratory school to university/community constituencies, providing university outreach to child and family clientele, participating in fund-development efforts; and writing reports.

Rationale. The strongest argument that the directorship is legitimate faculty work resides in identifying and documenting the position as an essential experience in the education of child development, family studies, and early childhood education majors. A secondary argument is that the collaboration with the community provides opportunities for outreach education to the public, for the professional development of early childhood professionals in the community, for strengthening ties between the university and the community, and for developing and testing new models for early childhood education.

Issues in Documentation. Issues involved concern the non-traditional teaching role of the director, dual responsibilities to the department and to clientele, establishing the degree of performance excellence, determining the unique contributions of the program (as opposed to non-university programs that might be used as alternatives), and identifying the impact of the director apart from the totality of the laboratory faculty/staff. The position is sometimes difficult to describe on a curriculum vitae for promotion and tenure.

Guidelines for Documentation. Documentation is needed up front concerning the nature of the academic appointment and the department/college expectations of the faculty member. A teaching portfolio should be constructed which could include videotapes of teaching activities and student/parent evaluations of these activities as appropriate. The faculty member should keep a diary of "critical instances" — times where faculty expertise is required. The demand for service figures and funds generated help to establish the impact of the program. Program evaluations by external evaluators (accreditation site visits) help to establish the level of excellence. The teaching portfolio also should include a statement of how the faculty member's activity is congruent with the department/college mission and the mission of the field of study. Research related to model programming can lead to juried presentations, refereed journal articles, chapters in books, and other publications that provide additional documentation.

Curriculum Development for Secondary Programs

Description. A home economics education faculty member is involved in developing a module on work and family life for inclusion in the state's secondary family and consumer sciences education programs. This activity involves reviewing literature on work and family life; working with an advisory committee consisting of subject matter faculty, state department of education personnel, and school administrators and others; coordinating the writing activities of working groups of teachers; field testing the curriculum in the schools; and developing appropriate assessment measures to accompany the curriculum.

Rationale. Working on curriculum development for family and consumer sciences programs at the secondary level is important for two reasons. Developing a sound curriculum can lead to an increase in the number of students who choose to major in family and consumer sciences at the college and university level. Curricular materials that are theoretically sound in terms of subject matter as well as teaching and learning methodology are essential to the field. These curricular materials often provide the first educational experiences many individuals have with the diversity of programs in family and consumer sciences.

Issues in Documentation. Issues to consider include whether or not this activity will be recognized as important at the college and university levels. Bringing this kind of activity before a college or university promotion and tenure committee could be a potential problem because it is not a traditional activity for faculty outside teacher education.

Guidelines for Documentation. The curricular materials themselves would be credible evidence of scholarship as would data on the number of schools that have adopted the curriculum. Feedback from high school teachers, principals, and community members in the form of letters or newspaper articles attesting to the value of the curriculum would be useful as well.

Many statewide curriculum development projects are funded through a competitive process. Success in obtaining funding can provide valuable documentation for the activity. Other forms of documentation include peer reviews. Some journals review curriculum materials and opportunities exist to present innovative curriculum materials at national professional association meetings. Selection of the materials to be showcased involves a juried process. Finally, faculty members involved in curriculum development projects should incorporate data collection efforts with the process that can lead to referred journal articles. For example, need assessment studies can be used as the basis for identifying critical content for inclusion.

APPENDIX A
BROADENING THE DEFINITION OF SCHOLARSHIP IN FAMILY AND CONSUMER SCIENCES

Examples from Foods and Nutrition, Textiles, Apparel and Fashion Merchandising, Home Economics Education, Consumer Resource Management, Family Relations and Child Development
Task Force on Defining Scholarly Work, February, 1992

The Task Force concluded that scholarship can occur within a broad scope of faculty work, including (but not limited to) the examples that appear below. The examples are grouped to reflect the four kinds of scholarship suggested by Rice (1991).

Scholarship of Discovery:

Original research to advance knowledge includes naturalistic and laboratory studies. It may involve theory and model building, and may be interdisciplinary in nature. The research may be undertaken as a result of the interest of the researcher or may be commissioned by another entity. It must be documented and disseminated.

Integration of Ideas:

Ideas may be synthesized from a variety of sources or combined in innovative ways. They must be presented to the target audience in an accessible and permanent form. Curriculum development, textbook writing and creation of training manuals often fall into this category. Position papers, design exhibits, media productions and computer programs are other vehicles for presenting existing research in new and creative ways. Ideas may be integrated and presented through lay publications and trade journals as well as through professional publications.

Application of Knowledge:

Services to the community or profession frequently fall into this category of scholarship. They may consist of community development projects, internship coordination, direct services (e.g. counseling) to community members and advisory-board membership. Additional avenues for application include providing expert testimony and consultation. This category of scholarship includes professional service that requires disciplinary expertise, such as leadership in professional organizations, editing journals and newsletters, peer review of teaching/teaching materials and administration of laboratories and centers.

Transformation of Knowledge Through Teaching:

The interaction of the scholar as a learner and the student is central to this area of scholarship. The college or university classroom, off-campus forums, workshops, community extension courses and professional meetings are among places where this interaction may occur. Academic advisement and work with student organizations are other venues for interaction.

The Task Force agreed that broadening the definition of scholarship and refining evaluation techniques go hand in hand. While all of these activities may be scholarly, a particular activity may or may not meet scholarly criteria.

Task Force Members

Virginia Caples, Dean, Division of Home Economics, Alabama A&M University

Virginia Clark, Dean, College of Home Economics, South Dakota State University

Dixie Crase, Chair, Department of Home Economics, Memphis State University

Esther Glover-Fahm, Dean, School of Home Economics, University of Wisconsin, Stout

Kinsey Green, Dean, College of Home Economics, Oregon State University

L. Ross Hackler, Chair, Department of Home Economics, State University of New York

Darlene Kness, Chair, Department of Home Economics, Central State University

Connie Ley, Chair, Department of Home Economics, Illinois State University

Facilitators for the Task Force included:

E. Audrey Clark, Chair, Department of Family Environmental Sciences, California State University, Northridge

Susan Crockett, Dean, College of Human Development, Syracuse University

Marjorie Dibble, Associate Dean, College of Human Development, Syracuse University

APPENDIX B
MISSION AND VISION STATEMENTS DEVELOPED AT CALLOWAY GARDENS
1992

Mission for the Profession in Higher Education

The mission of the profession in higher education is to conduct research and provide educational programs that are integrative and are focused on reciprocal relationships among individuals, families, and their near environments toward improvement of the human condition within a dynamic world community.

Vision Statement

The (Home Economics) profession in higher education will be a leader for positive change from a multicultural perspective for individuals and families interfacing with multiple environments to meet the needs of a diverse and changing global community.

APPENDIX C
THE SCOTTSDALE MEETING
Positioning the Profession for the 21st Century
Scottsdale, AZ, October 21-24, 1993

A Conceptual Framework for the 21st Century

Recommended Name for the Profession: Family and Consumer Sciences
Sound Bite: Empowering Individuals . . . Strengthening Families . . . Enabling Communities
Unifying Focus: Family and Consumer Sciences uses an integrative approach to the relationships among individuals, families, and communities and the environment in which they function.

The profession takes leadership in:
▶ improving individual, family and community well-being;
▶ impacting the development, delivery and evaluation of consumer goods and services;
▶ influencing the development of policy;
▶ shaping societal change; thereby enhancing the human condition.

The profession is concerned with:
▶ the strength and vitality of families;
▶ the development and use of personal, social and material resources to meet human needs;
▶ the physical, psychosocial, economic and aesthetic well-being of individuals and families;
▶ the role of individuals and families as consumers of goods and services;
▶ the development of home and community environments that are supportive of individuals and families;
▶ the design, management and use of environments;
▶ the design, use of and access to current and emerging technologies;
▶ the critique, development and implementation of policies that support individuals, families and communities.

Basic Beliefs
We believe in:
▶ families as the fundamental social unit;
▶ a life-span approach to individual and family development;
▶ meeting individual and family needs within and outside the home;

- ▶ diversity that strengthens individual, family and community well-being;
- ▶ the right to educational opportunities for all individuals to enhance their intellectual development and maximize their potential;
- ▶ strong subject matter specializations with a commitment to integration;
- ▶ the use of diverse modes of inquiry;
- ▶ education as a lifelong process.

Planning Assumptions

As the profession positions itself for the 21st century, it will:

- ▶ build upon its historical and philosophical foundations;
- ▶ be visionary, visible and influential;
- ▶ build upon the sciences, arts and humanities;
- ▶ use research as a basis for professional practice;
- ▶ prepare individuals for careers and professions;
- ▶ strive for professional competence and continuing professional development;
- ▶ incorporate a global perspective.

Professional Practice

- ▶ We focus on the discovery, integration and application of knowledge.
- ▶ We use analytical/empirical, interpretive and critical sciences and modes of inquiry.
- ▶ We integrate knowledge across subject and functional areas.
- ▶ We use a systems approach in professional practices. We provide services along a continuum from prevention to intervention with prevention being our primary focus.
- ▶ We address both emerging and persistent, perennial concerns of individuals and families by building strong specializations, bringing specialists together and establishing partnerships of professionals and consumers.
- ▶ We establish partnerships with other professionals and organizations to accomplish mutual goals.
- ▶ We practice from an ethical base.
- ▶ We advocate on behalf of individuals, families, consumers and communities through professional practice.
- ▶ We promote leadership and organizational development.
- ▶ We practice our profession within the context of:
  - — education
  - — government
  - — research
  - — extension
  - — business
  - — communications
  - — health and human services
  - — community based organizations
  - — homes

Outcomes

The outcomes of our professional practice are:

▶ the enhancement of social, cognitive, economic, emotional and physical health and well-being of individuals and families;

▶ the empowerment of individuals and families to take charge of their lives, to maximize their potential, and to function independently and interdependently;

▶ the enhancement of the quality of the environment in which individuals and families function.

ABOUT THE REPORT

This report was written for the Council of Administrators of Family and Consumer Sciences (CAFCS). The content was drawn from the aggregate of Task Force and Annual Meeting findings and discussions on the topic of faculty roles and rewards that were sponsored by the Council between February, 1992 and August, 1994 in conjunction with the Center for Instructional Development at Syracuse University (CID). The thoughts expressed in the report are those of the Council, rather than the personal opinions of the authors.

The authors represented CAFCS to CID over the course of the project. Dr. Audrey Clark, who is Chair of the Department of Family Environmental Sciences at California State University, Northridge, was liaison to CID since the inception of the project. Dr. Jerelyn Schultz, Dean of the College of Human Ecology at The Ohio State University, participated in the 1993 Summer Conference at the Minnowbrook Conference grounds sponsored by CID.

A number of other people made unique contributions to the report. The Council would particularly like to express its appreciation to Dr. Robert Diamond, Vice-Chancellor for Instructional Development, Syracuse University, who was Director of the CID project. Dean Susan Crockett and Associate Dean Marjorie Dibble, College for Human Development at Syracuse University served as Task Force facilitators. Dr. Ross Hackler, State University of New York College at Oneonta represented CAFCS at the CID Conference in 1992. Dr. Virginia Clark, President and Dr. George Wise, Treasurer of the 1994-1995 CAFCS Board reviewed the report and made suggestions that enhanced the content. □

APPENDIX

·

NEA Statement on Faculty Reward Structures*

The Changing Landscape

Higher education in the United States is at a crossroads and will undergo a major restructuring in the next decade. This is a time of problems, challenges, and opportunities for the higher education community. The expansion of knowledge, information, and new technologies have the potential to change the curriculum, pedagogy, and the ways students learn, notions and definitions of faculty workload and accountability. The changing demands on faculty and students all call for innovation. At the same time, there is unprecedented criticism of higher education institutions alleging they are neglecting teaching, ignoring the needs of students, and lacking accountability for the use of public funds. Restructuring is being pushed by a fiscal crisis that has resulted from a stagnation or decline of state support for higher education and spiraling fees and tuition to make up for decreased funding.

America's higher education system is recognized as the world's premier system, attracting students from all over the world. Clark Kerr notes that: "In the course of the twentieth century the United States has established clear leadership in the world of science and scholarship." Kerr further notes that during the period between 1960 and 1980 higher education underwent a "great transformation": from a system of nearly 50 percent private to one that is 80 percent public; from a system comprised of research universities to one dominated by comprehensives and community colleges and, from a professoriate of 235,000 to 685,000 with one-third unionized. Enrollments increased from 3.5 million to over 12 million students, increasing the amount of money spent on federal student aid. The growth of community colleges provided expanded access to non-traditional students who wanted to attend college.

During the decade of the eighties, enrollment grew to over 13.5 million students, and dramatic changes occurred among the student population so that today: women are the majority of undergraduate students; 43 percent of the students are over the

* The two million member National Education Association has over 130 years of experience in education advocacy. It supports the efforts of its members to safeguard intellectual freedom, tenure, the right to a voice in academic governance, and professional integrity. This statement was approved by the NEA Executive Committee in June 1994. It is reprinted with the permission of the NEA.

age of 25; minority students make up approximately 20 percent of the enrollment; there are more students in two-year schools than four-year; more students live off-campus than in dormitories; and many students attend part-time. Increasing numbers of part-time faculty have been hired, especially in the two-year colleges.

PUBLIC CRITICISM OF HIGHER EDUCATION

In recent years, the nature, quality, and purpose of higher education have been called into question by the public, including considerable discussion and debate about faculty workload. There has been criticism in the popular, policy, and academic literature about the faculty's supposed allocation of effort toward research and graduate education, away from undergraduate instruction and student advising. Unfortunately, the discourse has too often represented research university conditions as the norm rather than take into account the full range of doctoral, comprehensive, liberal arts, and two-year institutional missions. That discourse is also related to a broader critique of inefficiency in higher education, with the common criticism being that colleges and universities are charging "more for less." That context has translated into state legislative and institutional efforts to increase faculty teaching responsibilities, generally defined as contact hours with undergraduates. Serious discussion of such proposals is now widespread across the country. However, rarely has the criticism of higher education directly considered student learning, though a recent Wingspread report issued in the fall of 1993, *An American Imperative,* concluded: "The simple fact is that some faculties and institutions certify for graduation too many students who cannot read and write very well, too many whose intellectual depth and breadth are unimpressive, and too many whose skills are inadequate in the face of the demands of contemporary life."

TEACHING AND RESEARCH

In spite of the fact that there is a great deal of diversity of missions among the different types of institutions, there has been a tendency to evolve into the model of the research universities. The result is that faculty workload pressures have increased and reward structures increasingly require research and publication for tenure, promotion, and merit pay. In a 1989 National Survey of Faculty conducted by the Carnegie Foundation for the Advancement of Teaching, forty-two percent of all respondents strongly agreed with the statement, "In my department it is difficult for a person to achieve tenure if he or she does not publish." In a similar study conducted in 1969 only 21 percent strongly agreed. The institutions with the largest increase in agreement were the comprehensive institutions, where 6 percent in 1969 strongly agreed compared to 43 percent in 1989. This shift in emphasis over the last two decades has resulted in a workload increase for faculty, especially in the comprehensive institutions, which are often defined as teaching institutions, and where faculty have traditionally had heavier teaching loads than the research universities. There was no reduction in the teaching load when the comprehensives shifted their priorities to include research and publication by teaching faculty. At the research institutions, the pressures for change have led to demands for differentiated teaching loads, with those judged "unproductive" assigned higher teaching loads than those receiving large research grants or publishing in the highest status journals. This has led to arbitrary judgments of "productivity" and conflict between and within departments. It also suggests teaching is not valued.

A CALL FOR BALANCE

This discussion is *not* about diminishing or devaluing the role of research at the institutions. Such research has resulted in major discoveries and inventions. Faculty research has made the U. S. a leader in areas such as medicine, aerospace, computer theory and technology, genetics, economics, physics, and a multitude of other disciplines. The faculty's ability to continue to present up-to-date scholarship in the classroom is strengthened by the involvement of students in research projects and by the work of other faculty in research labs. A recent Research Brief published by the American Council on Education notes that "expenditures for scientific research and development (R&D) have long been seen as a vital component of a nation's economic strength and international standing." The report concludes that universities "play an important role in the national economy" not only through their contribution to R&D but also because they perform most of the nation's basic research. The funding for this, however, is heavily concentrated in the research universities.

In 1990, the publication of *Scholarship Reconsidered: Priorities of the Professoriate* by Ernest Boyer of the Carnegie Foundation began a reexamination throughout higher education of faculty work and how it should be evaluated and rewarded. Boyer challenges higher education to "break out of the tired old teaching versus research debate" and to redefine scholarship to "give more options to professors and better service to students." The report strongly reaffirms the importance of research, but notes that a "wide gap now exists between the myth and the reality of academic life. Almost all colleges pay lip service to the trilogy of teaching, research, and service, but when it comes to making judgments about professional performance, the three rarely are assigned equal merit." Further, to "define the work of the professoriate narrowly — chiefly in terms of the research model — is to deny many powerful realities. It is our central premise, therefore, that other forms of scholarship — teaching, integration, and application must be fully acknowledged and placed on a more equal footing with discovery."

Boyer calls for diversity among the institutions: "In building a truly diverse higher learning system, let's have great research centers where undergraduate instruction *also* will be honored. Let's have campuses where the scholarship of teaching is a central mission. Let's have colleges and universities that promote integrative studies as an exciting mission through a core curriculum, through interdisciplinary seminars, and through team teaching. And let's also have colleges and universities that give top priority to the scholarship of application, institutions that relate learning to real life—in schools, in hospitals, in industry, and in business — much as the land-grant colleges worked with farmers. What we are calling for is *diversity with dignity* in American higher education — a national network of higher learning institutions in which each college and university takes pride in its own distinctive mission and seeks to complement rather than imitate the others. Why should one model dominate the system?"

Community colleges, for example, have teaching at the core of their mission. These institutions also have a tradition of responding to community needs, have a commitment to fulfilling the goal of life-long learning, and of serving a diverse population of students. Many of these campuses serve as vehicles for economic development through training programs, re-skilling for displaced workers, training for new industry needs, re-entry training for women returning to the workforce, and opportunity for entrance into the middle class by our economically disadvantaged citizens and immigrants. The community colleges have traditionally served three functions — transfer programs to four-year campuses, personal enrichment, and job training. Teaching improvement efforts abound in these institutions. Reward structures for participation and implementation of teaching improvement strategies need to expand. While evaluation may vary among community colleges in its relationship to teaching improvement, it is important to reward faculty for teaching improvement efforts. Society clearly values the education and training of its citizenry and workforce that is provided by community colleges. This appreciation needs to find embodiment in a better reward structure for faculty.

CHANGING THE REWARD STRUCTURES

Since the publication of *Scholarship Reconsidered* there has been a movement to change the reward structures in higher education. Eugene Rice, from Antioch College (recently appointed the head of AAHE's faculty reward project) proposed an alternative concept for scholarly work. Drawing on the work of Boyer and others, Rice proposed four components to scholarship: (1) the advancement of knowledge — original research; (2) the integration of knowledge — integrating research into new patterns and relationships; (3) the application of knowledge — professional practice related to a research field; and (4) the transformation of knowledge through teaching. Rice concludes: "What is being called for is a broader, more open field where these different forms of scholarship can interact, inform, enrich one another, and faculty can follow their interests, build on their strengths, and be rewarded for what they spend most of their scholarly energy doing." Other organizations have called for more attention to teaching, including the American Association for Higher Education, the National Endowment for the Humanities, and the Association of American Colleges. Many of the discipline associations in higher education are in the midst of changing their criteria for tenure and promotion, as are individual campuses. In 1991, with funding from the Lilly Foundation and the Fund for the Improvement of Postsecondary Education, the Center for Instructional Development at Syracuse University began working with twenty disciplinary associations to expand their definition of scholarship and to look at faculty reward structures for the year 2000 and beyond.

NEA's POSITION

NEA is prepared to place itself in the forefront of a serious dialogue about changing faculty reward structures in higher education and to respond forcefully to charges that have been lodged against higher education faculty. There are two popular myths to be dispelled about higher education faculty. The first is that faculty members don't work hard enough. Every recent study of faculty workload, both nationally and in specific states, shows clearly that faculty members work an average of 53 hours per week and that workloads have increased steadily in the last decade. Community college faculty members spend 71 percent of their time spent each week on teaching, while faculty members at comprehensive institutions spend 62 percent of each week on teaching. Even faculty members at the research universities spend 43 percent of their time on teaching, compared to 29 percent on research.

The second myth is that faculty members don't value teaching and neglect their students. On the contrary, surveys show that faculty care most about teaching. The 1989 Carnegie Foundation study asked faculty, "Do your interests lie primarily in Research or in Teaching?" Among all respondents, 70 percent reported teaching was their primary interest; in the comprehensive institutions 77 percent chose teaching; and in the two-year colleges, 93 percent. In another national survey conducted in 1989 by UCLA, a large majority of faculty (90 percent) defined teaching as their principal activity, rated being a good teacher as either an "essential" or "very important goal" (98 percent, compared to 59 percent for "engage in research"), and reported their interests lie "very heavily in teaching," or "leaning toward teaching" (72 percent valued teaching compared to 28 percent for research). There were significant numbers of faculty who reported they "strongly" (27 percent) or "somewhat" (44 percent) agree that research demands interfere with teaching effectiveness.

Faculty reward systems must have variety and reflect the realities of faculty work. Recent studies indicate there is an inverse relationship between faculty pay and the amount of time spent teaching. With the exception of the two-year colleges, the more time faculty members spend teaching, the less they are paid. The reward systems for faculty pay, promotion, and resources in four-year colleges and universities are too heavily weighed toward published research. This is true even in institutions where teaching and service are, or should be, more central to the institution's stated mission than research. To evaluate teaching success, we must develop better, mutually agreeable methods to document good teaching, including teaching portfolios, videotaped classes, peer and student evaluation, review of course outlines, reading lists, exams, and student success. Appropriate education and training should be provided to all parties in the evaluation process. We must also recognize the differences in disciplines and missions of the institutions.

Therefore, the NEA endorses the following and believes that the goals below can only be achieved with fairness, equity and professional dignity through strengthened shared governance, and collective bargaining:

1. NEA's policy on Evaluation and Promotion in Higher Education is found in NEA Resolution D-18 which provides as follows:

    The National Education Association affirms the importance of teaching in institutions of higher education and believes, therefore, that research and publication ought not to be the only criteria on which higher education faculty are evaluated and/or promoted.

The Association further believes that its higher education members must be allowed to determine through collective bargaining process the methods by which they are evaluated and promoted.

2. Since teaching takes up the majority of faculty work time, it should be rewarded accordingly. Campuses need to recognize good teaching through appropriate evaluation systems that include student, faculty, and administrator input. Teaching, as a noble enterprise, should be justly rewarded.

3. The reward structures should reflect the mission of the institution. Institutions whose mission is teaching undergraduate students should reward good teaching. Institutions whose mission is community outreach should reward service. The proper balance between teaching, service, and research is contingent on faculty and administration agreement upon the institutional mission of the particular campus.

4. The faculty and the department should be a party to the development of the mission statement for the campus and the revision of reward systems to reflect that mission. The balance of the workload should reflect the discipline and mission of the campus. Service is a major, but often misunderstood and underrated component of the triad of research, teaching and service. Higher education faculty contribute significantly to the effective and efficient operations of their institutions. They also impact their communities, states, and the nation through their service activities.

5. Reward systems should be flexible and allow faculty to pursue and seek advancement in a variety of ways, and should be flexible enough to allow faculty to pursue different interests at different times in their careers. Evaluation should be linked to performance of assigned responsibilities, career growth and development, as well as tenure, promotion, and renewal. The evaluations should be formative to encourage risk-taking and growth.

6. Many institutions do not evaluate temporary or adjunct faculty. Temporary faculty should be evaluated and given assistance with teaching techniques. New faculty should be given a comprehensive orientation to the institution, its mission and goals, and the role of faculty.

7. Mentoring programs should be in place on all campuses to assist new faculty with the tenure and socialization process. Mentoring programs should further the affirmative action goals related to advancing the teaching and research opportunities

for all faculty.

8. The development of better ways to document and evaluate good teaching should be a high priority. Higher education should do a better job of promoting the use of effective teaching techniques for graduate assistants, adjuncts, and permanent faculty, especially techniques related to reaching nontraditional students.

9. Campuses need to dedicate more resources to faculty development and to providing access to current instructional technology.

10. The academic or instructional department should be the linchpin in the goal-setting. The department is the place where the institutional goals directly intersect with the faculty work and the students. There is a need to recognize that the disciplines will vary in their approach to the mix of teaching, research and service. For example, chemistry has traditionally valued professional service and outreach along with research; geography has placed a heavy emphasis on teaching; creative products have been valued in the arts. Attention should be paid to the criteria being developed by the disciplines, and efforts should be made to work collaboratively with the discipline associations. □

REFERENCES AND RESOURCES

Arreola, Raoul A. *Developing a Comprehensive Faculty Evaluation System.* Bolton, MA: Anker, 1995.

> A practical handbook of protocols, worksheets, and assessment instruments that can be used in developing a faculty evaluation system. Also includes a number of case studies and a formula for determining merit pay.

Bowker, Lee H., Hans O. Mauksch, Barbara Keating, and Dennis R. McSeveney. *The Role of the Department Chair.* Washington, DC: American Sociological Association Teaching Resources Center, 1992.

> A useful guide for department chairs in sociology having application for other academic areas, as well. Discusses the role of chair as advocate and includes a section on special issues related to women serving in this role. Case studies provide interesting situations to consider.

Boyer, Ernest L. *Scholarship Reconsidered: Priorities for the Professoriate.* Princeton, NJ: Carnegie Foundation for the Advancement of Teaching, 1990.

> An ideal introduction to rethinking the definition of scholarly or professional work. While not all departments or disciplines may find the schema developed by Eugene Rice and Ernest Boyer appropriate, this work has provided a basis for much of the change in thinking about scholarship at colleges and universities. An excellent volume for launching campus discussion.

Braskamp, Larry A., and John C. Ory. *Assessing Faculty Work.* San Francisco: Jossey-Bass, 1994.

> Describes the expanding role of faculty assessment and the limitations of present methods and discusses how assessment can be used to improve the quality of teaching and learning. A discussion of the scholarly nature of faculty work is followed by useful sections on relating institutional expectations to assessment and on collecting and organizing evidence of teaching effectiveness.

Centra, John A. *Reflective Faculty Evaluation.* San Francisco: Jossey-Bass, 1994.

> An extension of his 1979 publication on determining faculty effectiveness, with a significant addition in the area of teaching portfolios, self-reporting, and the

role of colleagues and chairs in teaching evaluation. Includes an in-depth review of specific techniques and sources of information.

_____, Robert C. Froh, Peter Gray, and Leo M. Lambert. *A Guide to Evaluating Teaching for Promotion and Tenure.* Syracuse, NY: Center for Instructional Development, Syracuse University, 1987.

A practical guide that discusses what should be evaluated to assess teaching effectiveness. Sources of information are discussed and various data collection techniques are described. Examples are provided, along with the advantages and limitations of the various approaches.

Cochran, Leslie H. *Publish or Perish: The Wrong Issue.* Cape Girardeau, MO: StepUp Publications, 1992.

Focuses on the integration of teaching and scholarship. Includes recommendations to academic leaders on actions they can take to reestablish the importance of teaching on their campuses.

Diamond, Robert M. *Preparing for Promotion and Tenure Review.* Bolton, MA: Anker, 1995.

Designed to help faculty prepare for promotion and tenure review. Makes specific recommendations about questions to ask and the materials to provide. Includes a number of illustrative examples on preparing documentation.

_____. *Serving on Promotion and Tenure Committees: A Faculty Guide.* Bolton, MA: Anker, 1994.

A handbook for faculty serving on promotion and tenure committees. This guide outlines problem cases and provides committees with procedural recommendations designed to make the process fair to the candidate and easier on the committee.

_____, and Bronwyn E. Adam. *Recognizing Faculty Work: Reward Systems for the Year 2000.* New Directions in Higher Education, no 81. San Francisco: Jossey-Bass, 1993.

Provides a model for relating the faculty reward system to institutional priorities as they are enacted at the level of the academic unit. Includes a number of campus case studies and discusses intrinsic rewards and the professional portfolio.

Edgerton, Russell, Patricia Hutchings, and Kathleen Quinlan. *The Teaching Portfolio: Capturing the Scholarship in Teaching.* Washington, DC: American Association for Higher Education, 1991.

> Provides a rationale for the teaching portfolio, and discusses documents that might be presented. Includes examples of teaching-related materials and reflective statements and discusses the process of getting started in the use of this approach to documenting teaching.

Elman, Sandra E., and Sue Marx Smock. *Professional Service and Faculty Rewards: Toward an Integrated Structure.* Washington, DC: National Association of State Universities and Land-Grant Colleges, 1985.

> Addresses the issues related to recognizing professional service in the faculty reward system. Provides a rationale for including this type of activity in the recognition system and describes the range of faculty work that falls in this area.

Entering the Profession: Advice for the Untenured. Washington, DC: National Education Association, 1994.

> Designed for faculty on unionized campuses, this guidebook pays particular attention to the formal appeal process. (Single copies available at no cost from the NEA.)

Farmer, J.A., and S.F. Schomberg. *A Faculty Guide for Relating Public Service to the Promotion and Tenure Review Process.* Champaign, IL: University of Illinois at Urbana-Champaign, Office of Continuing Education and Public Service, 1993.

> Designed to help UIUC faculty involved in public service activities relate their professional work to the mission statement of this institution. A good example of what could be provided to faculty. (Single copies available at no cost from the UIUC Office of Continuing Education and Public Service.)

Hutchings, Patricia. *Campus Use of the Teaching Portfolio: Twenty-Five Profiles.* Washington, DC: American Association for Higher Education, 1993.

> Detailed accounts of what twenty-five campuses are doing with teaching portfolios. Each profile answers a common set of questions, including what the portfolio consists of, how it is evaluated, and the impact the process has had on teaching and learning. Includes public and private institutions of various sizes and missions.

Seldin, Peter. *Successful Use of the Teaching Portfolio.* Bolton, MA: Anker, 1993.
Primarily for administrators-chairs to presidents, this volume presents the use of the teaching portfolio in an institutional context. Discusses implementation of a campus-wide portfolio assessment plan for faculty as an integral part of the reward system. Includes sample portfolios.

_____ . *The Teaching Portfolio.* Bolton, MA: Anker, 1991.
This faculty guide describes a rationale for the use of a teaching portfolio and provides detailed recommendations for assembling such a dossier. Includes a number of representative samples.

_____ , and associates. *How Administrators Can Improve Teaching.* San Francisco: Jossey-Bass, 1990.
Thirteen nationally prominent educators talk about improving teaching by developing institutional policies and practices that support and reward good teaching.

Tierney, William G., and Robert A. Rhoads. *Enhancing Promotion, Tenure, and Beyond: Faculty Socialization as a Cultural Process.* ASHE-ERIC Higher Education Report, no. 6. Washington, DC: The George Washington University, 1993.
Discusses how faculty values are shaped and how these values are reflected in faculty roles. Discusses tenure and promotion as part of a socialization process. Includes an interesting case study illustrating how action could have been taken by a candidate and by others in the department to avoid a negative decision.

Wergin, Jon F. *The Collaborative Department: How Five Campuses Are Inching Toward Cultures of Collective Responsibility.* Washington, DC: American Association for Higher Education, 1994.
Includes five detailed cases illustrating different approaches to shifting the focus of incentives and rewards from the individual faculty member to the department. Pulls together central issues that the five institutions, different though they are, confront about collective responsibility. The institutions are Kent State, Rochester Institute of Technology, Syracuse University, University of California-Berkeley, University of Wisconsin-Madison.

Whicker, Marcia Lynn, Jennie Jacobs Kronenfeld, and Ruth Ann Strickland. *Getting Tenure.* Newbury Park, CA: Sage Publications, 1993.

>   Traces the steps in the traditional tenure and promotion process. This volume includes major emphasis on the politics of promotion and tenure.

DISCIPLINARY STATEMENTS

American Academy of Religion. "Religious Studies and the Redefining Scholarship Project: A Report of the AAR Ad Hoc Committee on 'Defining Scholarly Work'." Syracuse, NY, 1993. Photocopy.

American Chemical Society. "Report of the American Chemical Society Task Force on the Definition of Scholarship in Chemistry." Washington, DC, January 1993. Photocopy.

American Historical Association. *Redefining Historical Scholarship: Report of the American Historical Association Ad Hoc Committee on Redefining Scholarly Work.* Washington, DC: AHA, 1994.

Association for Education in Journalism and Mass Communication. "Report of the Association for Education in Journalism and Mass Communication on the Definition of Scholarship in Journalism." Gainesville, FL, November 19, 1992. Photocopy.

Association of American Geographers. *Toward a Reconsideration of Faculty Roles and Rewards in Geography.* Washington, DC: AAG, 1994.

Council of Administrators of Family and Consumer Sciences. *Recognition and Rewards in the Family and Consumer Sciences.* Northridge, CA: CAFCS, 1994.

Joint Policy Board for Mathematics. *Recognition and Rewards in the Mathematical Sciences: Report of the Joint Policy Board for Mathematics Committee on Professional Recognition and Rewards.* Providence, RI: American Mathematical Society, 1994.

Laidlaw, William K., Jr. "Defining Scholarly Work in Management Education." St. Louis, MO, American Assembly of Collegiate Schools of Business, July 1992. Photocopy.

National Education Association. *NEA Statement on Faculty Reward Structures.* Washington, DC: National Education Association, 1994.

National Office for Arts Accreditation in Higher Education. *The Work of Arts Faculties in Higher Education.* Reston, VA: National Office for Arts Accreditation in Higher Education, 1994.

About AAHE and Its
Forum on Faculty Roles & Rewards

What Is AAHE?

The American Association for Higher Education (AAHE) is a national organization of more than 8,500 individuals dedicated to improving the quality of higher education. AAHE members share two convictions: that higher education should play a more central role in national life, and that each of our institutions can be more effective. AAHE helps to translate those convictions into action, through its programmatic activities, publications, and conferences. Member support enables AAHE to initiate special projects — such as the Forum on Faculty Roles & Rewards — on a range of issues to create effective change at the campus, state, and national levels.

Benefits of AAHE membership include subscriptions to *Change* magazine and the *AAHE Bulletin*; discounts on registration at AAHE's conferences; discounts on AAHE's publications; and more.

How Did the Forum Begin?

The myriad of calls to reinvent, redesign, or reengineer American higher education have all come to focus, sooner or later, on the role of faculty. The faculty is identified as the primary investment, the key resource, and sometimes, the biggest impediment to the change required to meet the critical needs of a new millennium. To address the critical issues related to the changing faculty role and the reward system, AAHE, with the support of the Fund for the Improvement of Postsecondary Education (FIPSE), established a special forum. The Forum on Faculty Roles & Rewards was inaugurated at its first national conference in January 1993.

What Is the Forum's Agenda?

The Forum began with the call to broaden higher education's view of scholarly work, and moved quickly to the question: "Can the quality of teaching and professional service — as well as research — be documented and rewarded in ways that are seen as legitimate by colleagues on one's own campus and beyond?" The central thrust of the Forum is to keep the extraordinarily constructive conversation about changing faculty roles moving ahead and to develop products that will assist faculty leaders and administrators in their efforts to make the individual work of faculty more congruent with the basic missions of their colleges and universities.

WHAT ARE THE KEY THEMES OF THE FORUM'S CURRENT WORK?

Honoring Different Forms of Scholarly Excellence: making teaching and service cosmopolitan and portable; AAHE/Stanford peer review of teaching project; evaluation of professional service; linking institutional priorities and reward systems (case studies); work with disciplinary and professional associations; Teaching Academy; redefining and rewarding the faculty advising role.

Organizing for Collaboration and Change: the department as the focus for change; learning to work collaboratively; faculty/administrative relationships; faculty rewards for institution building; strategies for change.

Rethinking Academic Careers: from career dependence to career resilience; new options for faculty; issues related to tenure; learning from other organizational careers; preparing the future professoriate; senior faculty; implications of a growing contingent workforce; coping with external careers of faculty; information technology and the changing role of faculty; transformation of the disciplines; use of practitioner faculty and the future of adult learning programs.

Taking Charge of Accountability: defining our own futures; communicating effectively with legislators and trustees; faculty workload and productivity; faculty role in assessment; post tenure review; new approaches to faculty compensation.

Faculty Responsibility for Public Life: from perceived emphasis on private advantage to concern for the common good; community service in teaching and research; recruiting and maintaining a diverse faculty; learning from the wisdom of practice.

WHAT RESOURCES AND SERVICES CAN THE FORUM PROVIDE?

The Forum sponsors national conferences on faculty roles and rewards, regional meetings, workshops, special projects, and publications. It works with key faculty, provosts, deans, and department chairs in reexamining faculty priorities, the structure of the academic career, and the reward system. Trustees of universities and colleges and legislators who work on issues of higher education policy are also involved.

Publications. AAHE offers several publications on the Forum's topics, including

The Collaborative Department: How Five Campuses Are Inching Toward Cultures of Collective Responsibility (by Jon Wergin) and *Making the Case for Professional Service* (by Ernest Lynton). For ordering information, contact the AAHE Pubs Order Desk (202/ 293-6440 x11).

HOW CAN I GET MORE INFORMATION ABOUT THE FORUM?

R. Eugene Rice is the *director* of the Forum. If you would like more information about the Forum, its meetings, and resources, contact the Forum's *program coordinator,* Pam Bender, Internet: aaheffrr@capcon.net.   ☐